10 TRAITS OF A MAN OF GOD

SERIES I

JAY T. HARRISON, SR.

WITH CO-AUTHOR APPEARANCES BY

ROBERT JAMISON
PARRIS BAKER
VINCENT SMITH
ALEXANDER BUTLER
WILLIAM MORSE
LES PARKER SR.
MICAH HARRISON
ROBERT KENION

FOREWARD BY: STANLEY K. SMITH

EDITED BY: PARRIS J. BAKER

10 Traits of a Man of God

Published by Grace 4 Purpose, Publishing Co. LLC

ISBN: 979-8-9879298-5-8

Editing by: Grace 4 Purpose, Publishing Co. LLC & Parris Baker, PhD.

Book cover design by Untouchable Designz and Consulting.

Printed and bound in the United States of America.

In Memory
of
Mekhi James Harrison

What Others are Saying about 10 Traits of a Man of God

"The chapter on The Faith of God captures the essence of not only what faith is, but how faith functions in the life of a believer. In his chapter, Pastor Butler explains with great clarity, simplicity and understanding of how faith comes, how it is challenged, but most of all how to give your faith a job and never give up on the promises of God. Powerful chapter within a powerful book of other great men that share their personal experiences. The Ten Traits of a Man of God will surely impact the life of every man that chooses to read this book."

- Elizabeth Butler, Pastor, Rhema Word Global

"I found the chapter on Prayer to be a resource of confirmation concerning the importance of our relationship with God. This chapter gives the reader great insights, with sufficient scriptural support, to the process of building a glorious relationship with God, Our Father. There is power in prayer!"

- Bishop L.C. & Elder Ellen Carter
  State Bishop of Pennsylvania, Full Gospel Baptist Church

"The book, 10 Traits of a Man of God, is an enjoyable read in the sense that all the authors are so transparent and pastoral in their writing, not to mention, so transparent in their faith."

- Aaron Kerr, PhD, Associate Professor, Gannon University
  Theology Department Program Director

"Exceptional work! I love how the authors drill down and become transparent. The illustrations, using familiar sports figures and contemporary imagery, invite the reader to get lost in the stories. The choices of scriptures as well as your commentary are very well integrated. I also believe the book is theological sound in your exegesis and narrative. A very accessible and relevant read."

- Charles E. Mock, DDiv., Retired Pastor
  Community Missionary Baptist Church

"10 Traits of a Man of God" is a phenomenal book written by men of God who have allowed God to use their testimonies and shortcomings to speak to the hearts of men around the world so that their lives may be saved for the purpose

of restoration in the lives of the broken hearted, homeless and those hungry for God that destiny may be fulfilled.

I want to specifically thank my husband, Pastor Jay T. Harrison Sr. for allowing God to use his pain and healed shortcoming to be a blessing in the lives of men who may struggle with infidelity. My dear, you are what I call "a man after God's own heart." Acts 13:22 "And when he had removed him, he raised up unto them David to be their king; to whom also he gave their testimony, and said, I have found David the son of Jesse, a man after mine own heart, which shall fulfil all my will."

I watched and prayed as many clergy, family, and friends distanced themselves from you during this storm, but my love I also watched as those warriors in the Kingdom drew near and prayed for and with you as your weakness was exposed; Bishop Stanley K. Smith, Bishop Kim A. Davis, Pastor Parris Baker, and Pastor Doris Presley each of you understood the assignment on this man of God's life and remained focused on the purpose in him and not the failure of the man.
The challenges of life have met us, weakened us, almost destroyed, and yes we thought internally killed us at times; but through the Grace of God everything meant to kill us God used to strengthen us. I am eternally grateful that God has restored you and is using you in a mighty way. I love you forever and will always "R.O.C.K" with you!

- Crystal D. Harrison, M.ED Pastor
  True Vine Missionary FGBC

DEDICATION

I want to say, "Thank you!" to our heavenly Father for forgiving me and for giving me the courage and wisdom to share the most challenging portion of my personal and private story. I am incredibly grateful to God for giving me the strength found in the liberty in Christ, made available to those who believed in His grace.

This book is dedicated to four men who were and remain significant godly mentors and leaders in my life. First, my father the late Bishop James L. Harrison, who was and still is my hero. He was the greatest example of a man of God in my life.

Second, my Pastor, Larry B. Surles, He taught me how to live the life of a Christian. Moreover, Pastor Surles taught me the importance of prayer, how to pray and why prayer should be a lifestyle. Pastor Surles you've made one of the greatest impacts on my life in teaching me how to commune with God in prayer.

Third, to Bishop Stanley K. Smith, who assumed the role as my spiritual father, not just in title, but in life experiences! You are and have proven yourself to truly be a father. You nourished my gift and calling and encouraged me to walk in my assignment as an intercessor. When I lost my sight, you rallied the entire State of Pennsylvania Full Gospel Fellowship of Pastors and local pastors in the City of Chester to create an emergency fund that would ensure that I received the surgery I needed. Bishop Smith, when I destroyed my marriage and failed in my assignment as pastor and moral leader of God's people, you were there to love me through the crisis, to correct and counsel me and to help restore my wife and I as one. Your agape "unconditional love" helped us navigate the healing and rebuilding trust process and encouraged us to receive grace from God to walk upright before Him again.

"God has not given up on David, so He won't give up on me."

Four, but certainly not least, I am indebted to each of the authors who have been in their own special way a true brother in Christ. Just as the Bible says in Proverbs 18: 24:

A man that hath friends must himself be friendly, But there is a friend that sticks closer than a brother.

And in Proverbs 17:17:

A friend loveth at all times, and a brother is born for adversity.

Each of you have given that to me.

Finally, and earnestly, to my wife Crystal Harrison. This writing project is so much about you, your love for God, for me, and for the people of God. Your willingness to allow the Holy Spirit to help you heal, to forgive me, and to extend a fresh opportunity to me to rebuild our trust. The love you showed me, like air to an oxygen-deprived man, has revived and restored me!

I love you baby! You are a blessing to me!

TABLE OF CONTENTS

Foreword

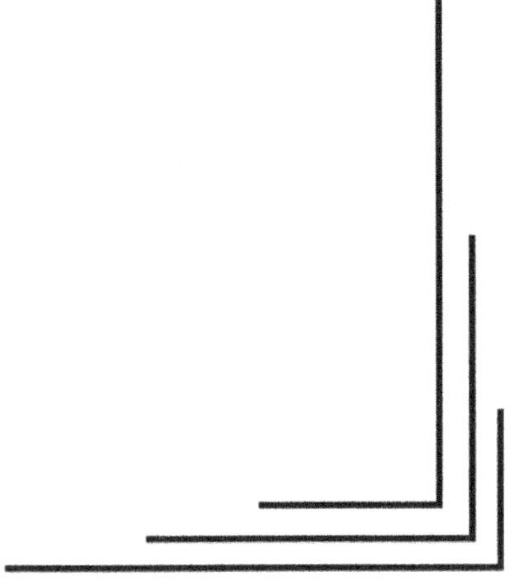

Stanley K. Smith

One of the most profound questions facing man is: Who is God? More appropriately – who is God to you? In Genesis 1:1 God introduces Himself as God: the creator. In the Gospels, He reveals Himself as God the Father, Son, and Holy Spirit. In the book of Revelation, He allows us to see Him as the God who was, and is, and is to come.

Throughout the 66 books of the Bible God demonstrates His love for His creation and His desire for man to enter a relationship, covenant, and fellowship with Him. Even when man arrogantly turns his back on God, our loving Father shows His love for us by seeking and drawing us unto himself. The birth, death, and resurrection of Jesus Christ is proof of His commitment and love for those He formed. Man's ultimate goal should be as Paul said: "to know Him, in the power of His resurrection and the fellowship of His suffering (Philippians 3:10.)

To that end Overseer Jay T. Harrison and eight other sages of God submit for your concertation the book, "The 10 Traits of a Man of God". This offering gives the reader the opportunity to examine and measure himself with the statute and standard of God for the purpose of submission and growth by the hand of God. If God's desire is for us to commune with Him, it would stand to reason that man's desire should be to know Him for the purpose of reflecting His Glory. The 10 Traits of a Man of God will afford you the opportunity for deep thought, reflective contemplation and continuous conversation with the God who not only created you but loves you and gave Himself for you. Allow these anointed authors to assist you as you look into the mirror of God's love and manifest the Glory of His magnificent presence.

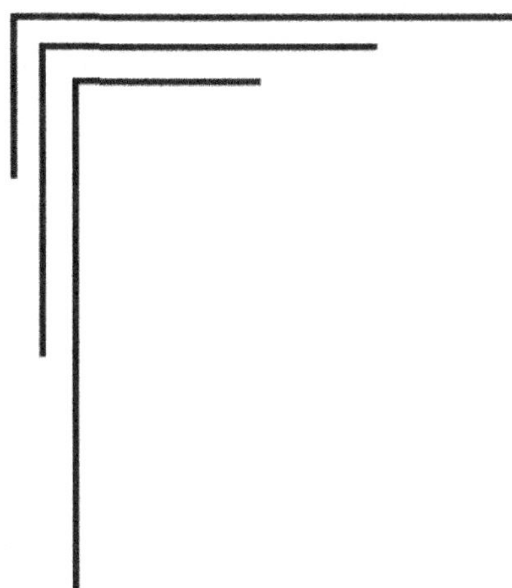

Introduction

Love: The Defining Characteristic of God

Parris Baker

The defining characteristic of God is love. Therefore, the defining characteristic of a man of God must also be love. 1 John 4: 7-11 makes this point very clearly:

> *Beloved, let us love one another: for love is of God; and everyone that loveth is born of God, and knoweth God. He that loveth not knoweth not God; for God is love. In this was manifested the love of God toward us, because that God sent his only begotten Son into the world, that we might live through him. Herein is love, not that we loved God, but that he loved us, and sent his Son to be the propitiation for our sins Beloved, if God so loved us, we ought also to love one another.*

Alistair Begg, Senior Pastor of Parkside Church, Cleveland, OH, was the keynote speaker of a conference and recounted this insightful story with the congregation:

> *A man who had recently died, was being interviewed by an angel receptionist of heaven. The interview went wildly back and forth. The Angel said, "Earlier today you were cussin' a guy out with your friend; you've never gone to bible study, you've never been baptized, and you know nothing about church membership, and yet (bewildered) you're here! You made it! What are you doing here? How did you make it into heaven?*
>
> *The man told the angel receptionist, "I don't know! "In astonishment the angel said, "Let me get my supervisor. The supervising angel began to ask the man a series of questions: Are you clear on the doctrine of Justification by Faith? The man said, "I never heard of it in my life!" What do you know about sanctification, glorification, and the purpose of propitiation? The man had no answers to the supervising angel's questions. So, the supervising angel asked one more question: On what basis are you here in heaven?*
>
> *The man answered, "The man on the middle cross said I could come."*

Wow! The man in the middle, Jesus Christ, said I could come. It really is that simple. Salvation is based on believing the finished works of Jesus Christ. Don't let people tell you that salvation is based on a bunch of rules that you must satisfy, before, during and after you receive Christ. I am guessing you will recognize John 3:16:

> *For God so loved the world, that he gave his only begotten Son, that whosoever believeth in him should not perish, but have everlasting life.*

Salvation is based, fundamentally, on a relationship with God through the *finished works* of Jesus Christ.

> *For by grace are ye saved through faith; and that not of yourselves: it is the gift of God: Not of works, lest any man should boast.* (Ephesians 2: 8-9)

The purpose of this book and the reason for our faith is found in our collective knowledge and belief in that scripture. We believe fervently that God is love and that God loves us. It is our hope that you read every word in every chapter in this book and listen to every story told. Each author has decided to be completely transparent to you and before the world, so that the love of God can be read and received by you. Don't miss the miracles.

And here's the hit! The love of God is eternal. God so loved us that we can live eternally with Him. Apostle sums up the love of God with a series of scriptures found in Romans 8: 31-39:

> *What shall we then say to these things? If God be for us, who can be against us? He that spared not his own Son, but delivered him up for us all, how shall he not with him also freely give us all things?*
>
> *Who shall lay anything to the charge of God's elect? It is God that justifieth. Who is he that condemneth? It is Christ that died, yea rather, that is risen again, who is even at the right hand of God, who also maketh intercession for us.*
>
> *Who shall separate us from the love of Christ? shall tribulation, or distress, or persecution, or famine, or nakedness, or peril, or sword? As it is written, For thy sake we are killed all day long; we are accounted as sheep for the slaughter.*
>
> *Nay, in all these things we are more than conquerors through him that loved us.*
>
> *For I am persuaded, that neither death, nor life, nor angels, nor principalities, nor powers, nor things present, nor things to*

> *come, Nor height, nor depth, nor any other creature, shall be able to separate us from the love of God, which is in Christ Jesus our Lord.*

We invite you to join us in discovering more about God and about ourselves. Your journey to learn the 10 Traits of a Man of God began when you picked up this book. We will talk again at the end of the book. Enjoy the journey!

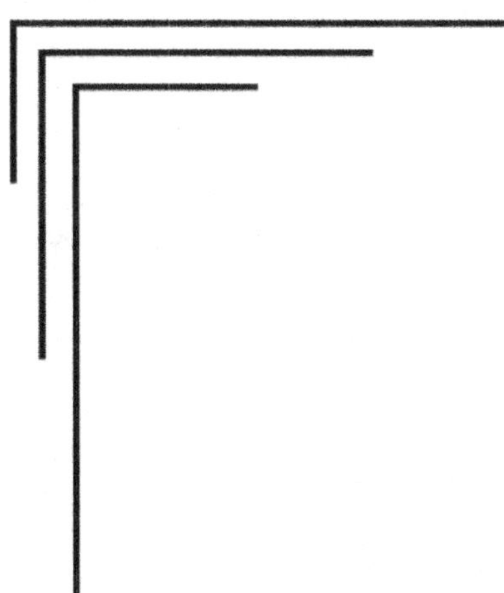

Chapter One

The Image of God

Parris Baker

The first characteristic presented in this book, *The Ten Characteristics of a Man of God*, is that man or humanity is made in the image of God. This phrase is found in Genesis 1: 26-28

> *Then God said, "Let us make man in our image, after our likeness. And let them have dominion over the fish of the sea and over the birds of the heavens and over the livestock and over all the earth and over every creeping thing that creeps on the earth." So God created man in his own image, in the image of God he created him; male and female he created them. And God blessed them; And God blessed them. And God said to them, "Be fruitful and multiply and fill the earth and subdue it and have dominion over the fish of the sea and over the birds of the heavens and over every living thing that moves on the earth."*

For centuries mankind has postulated the meaning of Imago Dei, the Latin term for being made in the image of God. I have decided to refer to the words of the prophet Luther Vandross (excerpts of A House is Not a Home) to gain some greater revelation, perspective, and insight into the meaning and purpose of being made in the image of God:

> A chair is still a chair, even when there's no one sittin' there. But
> a chair is not a house, and a house is not a home
> When there's no one there to hold you tight
> And no one there you can kiss goodnight.
>
> I'm not meant to live alone, turn this house into a home
> When I climb the stairs and turn the key
> Oh, please be there, still in love, still in love with me.

God is love (1 John 4: 8). Love is the single greatest identifying characteristic and attribute of His nature. Love is who God is and Love is what God does. Though He is Elohim (the God of Israel), the Triune God (God the Father, God the Son, and God the Holy Ghost) who is Self-Sufficient and Self-Reliant, needing nothing and no one, it is because He is love that He makes man uniquely like Himself, with similar attributes.

Only God is Omnipotent (all-powerful), Omnipresent (all-present everywhere), and Omniscient (all-knowing). However, like God, man can make sound and speak intelligently. We were created as *speaking spirits*, possessing dominion power and authority, and having the capacity to express and experience love.

God also declared and the prophet Luther Vandross reinforces in his recording, that it is not good for man to be alone. So, God anesthetized Adam, removed one of Adam's ribs and created woman to be a complimentary helper for Adam in fulfilling the commandments of God: to have dominion over fish, birds, and every living thing on the earth, to be fruitful, multiply and fill the earth, and to subdue the earth.

In the entire bible, from Genesis to Revelation, incredibly, you will not find this unbelievable blessing bestowed on any other creation. The Image of God or the *Imago Dei* is the expression of God's love for his human creation. The character and nature of God, that is the triune Godhead, God the Father, God the Son, and God the Holy Spirit, is manifested in the tripartite man, a composite of body, spirit, and soul. Genesis 2: 7 describes the creation of man:

> *then the* L*ORD* *God formed the man of dust from the ground and breathed into his nostrils the breath of life, and the man became a living creature.*

The image of God is not the fleshly body made from the dust of the ground, but the Spirit of God that was blown into the dirt that makes man a speaking-spirit, a living soul. As God is in communion and communication with Himself (Let Us make man…), He desires to be in communion and communication with mankind. God's love of and benevolence toward mankind is demonstrated in this phrase, Imago Dei. God did not confer His image to any other creation on earth. Everything that was created was created by God and for God, but none of God's other creations are like man. In fact, the universe was so amazed and marveled at God's creation of man that the writer of Psalm 8: 4-6 records:

> *what is man that you are mindful of him, and the son of man that you care for him? Yet you have made him a little lower than the heavenly beings and crowned him with glory and honor. You have given him dominion over the works of your hands; you have put all things under his feet,*

For the first five days of creation God created the heavens and earth and everything in the earth. On the sixth day of creation, God, who is sovereign and preeminent over all created things, made man (male and female), placed man into a perfectly created environment and immediately gave him/them dominion over all His works, the earth, and the fullness thereof. Adam and his wife and Eden were morally innocent, perfect, completely without evil and without death. To demonstrate that man had power and authority on the earth and the God would not usurp that authority of man God does the following:

> *Now out of the ground the LORD God had formed[f] every beast of the field and every bird of the heavens and brought them to the man to see what he would call them. And whatever the man called every living creature, that was its name*

Imago Dei means man was created to express love in relationships, through his actions and in his desire to fulfill specific expectations designed by God. Man was to be submitted to the authority and will of God. One evidence of love is obedience. God created male and female to have authority over all the earth, to be fruitful, multiply and to have dominion and was given one probationary statute:

> *And the LORD God commanded the man, saying, "You may surely eat of every tree of the garden, but of the tree of the knowledge of good and evil you shall not eat, for in the day that you eat of it you shall surely die."*

And for an undetermined period, Adam and his wife governed and presided over the earth and experienced unbroken fellowship with God. Before sin, man was a master over the environment and the environment was created to serve mankind. After sin, man became a servant and slave of sin and the earth. Genesis 3:17-19 reveals:

> *And to Adam he said, Because you have listened to the voice of your wife and have eaten of the tree of which I commanded you, 'You shall not eat of it,' cursed is the ground because of you; in pain you shall eat of it all the days of your life; thorns and thistles it shall bring forth for you; and you shall eat the plants of the field. By the sweat of your face, you shall eat bread, till you return to the ground, for out of it you were taken; for you are dust, and to dust you shall return."*

Imago Dei requires one to be intimately involved in a mutual relationship where care, concern, and love are reciprocated. Psychologists refer to the process where people develop specific positive or negative emotional bonds with other as attachment. What is important in the process of attachment is the synchrony of interaction; that is, interactions that are rhythmic, well timed, and mutually rewarding. When the interactions are synchronous, secure attachments are developed.

However, when the interactions are asynchronous the relationships may develop with heightened anxiety and fear, avoidant attitudes and behaviors, levels of disengagement and depression, and distorted perceptions of people. When one is unresponsive to the signals of distress, discomfort, or unmet needs or is inconsistent or uninvolved in the response to need gratification, less positive attachment occurs. In this manner relationships can be close and intimate or distant and empty. The type of relationship you have with God and with mankind depends on how close or how distant you are in the relationships.

When Adam sinned the image of God was not lost but became distorted and perverted. The image of God was distorted because man no longer reflected the flawless perfection and sinlessness nature of God. Moreover, Adam died spiritually, that is, he became separated from God. Due to sin man could no longer see or experience the flawless perfection and sinless nature of God. In the presence of a perfect God Adam and his wife hid themselves because they were afraid and recognized they were naked.

The fellowship between God and mankind was broken, due to Adam's disobedience. However, Adam's sin and disobedience did not change the love of God because God is love and God has declared, "For I the LORD do not change; therefore you, O children of Jacob, are not consumed. (Malachi 3: 6). Though sin had entered the world God so loved the world that He sent Jesus to redeem a lost, rebellious humanity from the sin of Adam:

> *For if, because of one man's trespass, death reigned through that one man, much more will those who receive the abundance of grace and the free gift of righteousness reign in life through the one-man Jesus Christ. Therefore, as one trespass led to condemnation for all men, so one act of righteousness leads to justification and life for all men. For as by the one man's disobedience the many were made sinners, so by the one man's obedience the many will be made righteous (Romans 5: 17-19).*

The Image of God as a Father

In Matthew 6 Jesus teaches the disciples to pray, providing them with the following instructions:

> *And when you pray, do not heap up empty phrases as the Gentiles do, for they think that they will be heard for their many words. Do not be like them, for your Father knows what you need before you ask him. Pray then like this:* ***Our Father*** *in heaven, hallowed be your name…* (emphasis added).

Of all names for God that Jesus could have chosen, including Elohim, El Shaddai, Adonai, I AM THAT I AM, Jehovah, and Yahweh, it appears that none are more characteristic of God than Abba or Father. Throughout his life Jesus always referred to God as Abba except one time on the cross when, *"Jesus cried out with a loud voice, saying, "Eli, Eli, lema sabachthani?" that is, "My God, my God, why have you forsaken me?"*

The name Abba has a special meaning. The common translation of the term Abba is that it means "Daddy." This translation is sentimental in its connotation of loving and caring father. However, the correct translation is more in line with the character of God and what He wants reflected in the character of man. Abba in Hebrew is spelled Aleph (א), Bet (ב), Bet (ב), Aleph (א).

Each letter in the Hebrew is a symbol and the symbol is used to help define the word. The first letter aleph (א) means unity, leader, master, teacher, progenitor, and protector. Transliteral meaning is our God who is one, united cares for His people/family below, initially the chosen nation of Israel. The second letter, Bet (ב), means tent, house, household or family, royal house, or temple. When placed together Abba means God is the leader, teacher and protector of the royal household or family.

As the Imago Dei, God wants men to be spiritual fathers, are men who are leaders of the homes and community. Spiritual fathers are men who have submitted their lives to God the Father; men who have been changed, transformed by the redemptive love of God, and turn to God in the training, instruction, and development of their children. Spiritual fathers are submitted sons who have yielded and have surrendered to the will or authority of Abba.

Submission is learned in the very act of submitting; therefore, submission requires faith, hope, and trust. You cannot beat someone into submission. Forced submission breeds resentment and rebellion (rebellious sons). Submission at its core is an act of love. It is essential that men and fathers learn submission by allowing God to teach and demonstrate love in them. It is through experiencing the love of God that men learn to love themselves, their wife or the mother of their children, and their children.

Spiritual fathers also believe in sacrificial love. Sacrifice means the forfeiture of something highly valued for the sake of one considered to have a greater value or claim. They are selfless in their perception of family, seeking to satisfy the needs of their wife or the mother of their children, and the needs of the children ahead of their own needs. Fathers create change in their children by depositing love in them. Fathers develop their children by anointing them, blessing them, and speaking life into them. They plan, prepare, and provide for their children and they pray for their children continually. They understand that they are responsible for their children and grandchildren.

The Image of God as a Son

For you did not receive the spirit of slavery to fall back into fear, but you have received the Spirit of adoption as sons, by whom we cry, "Abba! Father!" The Spirit himself bears witness with our spirit that we are children of God, and if children, then heirs—heirs of God and fellow heirs with Christ, provided we suffer with him in order that we may also be glorified with him.

The image of God was not lost because of sin but was distinctly unrecognizable in fallen man. Instead of seeking the will of the Father, mankind, through the inherited selfish nature of Adam, became self-indulgent, hedonistic, and a profligate, prodigal son. Beyond our inherited sin nature was the despair of death, the eternal separation from the love and grace of God the Father. However, God so loved the world that He gave his only begotten Son, Jesus. The believer knows that Jesus Christ became our sin that we might become the righteousness of God.

But why did God give His only begotten son? In the Imago Dei, the purpose of sons is to restore the original purpose of the Father. Through Jesus and His sacrifice of His innocent blood and the resurrection of His body our sin debt to God has been satisfied. Jesus declared from the cross, "It is finished!" or in the Greek, Tetelestai – the work is completed!

The work to complete the plan of salvation is finished. Now fallen man, by grace through faith, can once again experience salvation, eternal life, and uninterrupted fellowship with God the Father. But remember, God had an original plan for mankind, documented in Genesis 1: "*Be fruitful and multiply and fill the earth and subdue it and have dominion over the fish of the sea and over the birds of the heavens and over every living thing that moves on the earth."*

As believers, we are now the sons of God, empowered by the Holy Spirit to accomplish great works while we are alive. All mankind, you and me are born with purpose and equipped by God with all the resources necessary, spiritual and secular, to complete or fulfill that purpose.

> *And we all, with unveiled face, beholding the glory of the Lord, are being transformed into the same image from one degree of glory to another. For this comes from the Lord who is the Spirit (1 Corinthians 3:18)*

> *And we know that for those who love God all things work together for good, for those who are called according to his purpose. For those whom he foreknew he also predestined to be conformed to the image of his Son, in order that he might be the firstborn among many brothers (Romans 8:28-29)*

My prayer for the reader of this book:

Father God, give the reader of this book the courage to say what you tell them, to go where you lead them, and to sacrifice whatever is necessary that Your kingdom is established in this earth as it is in heaven.

Parris J. Baker, PhD., MSSA is an Associate Professor & Director, Social Work, Mortuary Science, and Gerontology Programs, Department of Criminal Justice & Social Work, at Gannon University. He received degrees in social work from Gannon University, Case Western Reserve University, Mandel School of Applied Social Sciences, and the University of Pittsburgh, School of Social Work, respectively. In 2011 Dr. Baker became the first African American faculty to earn rank and tenure at Gannon University. He most recently became a Jefferson Education Society Scholar-In-Residence in 2021 and a Harry T. Burleigh & Beyond Fellow in 2022.

An ordained elder, Dr. Baker is the senior pastor of Believers International Worship Center, Inc., and founder and director of Men of Valor Ministries, Inc., the Abba Fathers Program. Presently, Baker is a consultant with Strategic Consulting Partners charged with conducting a diversity, equity, and inclusion assessment of City of Erie administration, police and safety, public works, City Council, and City of Erie Stakeholders. Dr. Baker was also the 2022 Transition Team Chairman, Erie County Department of Human Services.

Research interests pursued by Dr. Baker include fathering and fatherhood, community and teenage violence, race and racism, and cultural diversity, justice, equity, and inclusion. Dr. Baker has co-authored fatherhood curricula: Foundations of Fatherhood, Long Distance Dads, and the Abba Fathers Program. The Fathers Workshop curriculum has been used by the Pennsylvania Department of Corrections, Erie Community Corrections Center (Pennsylvania Family Support Alliance), New Life City Mission, and in father support groups across the country.

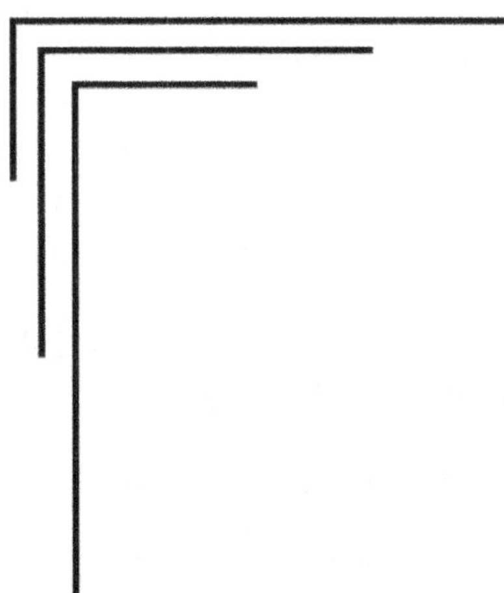

Chapter Two

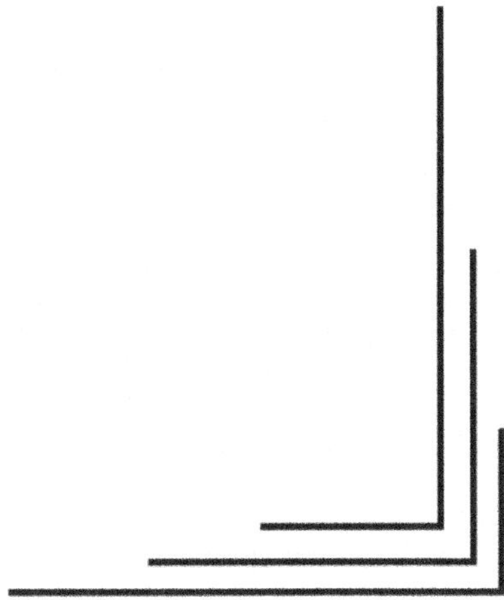

The Likeness of God

Parris Baker and Jay T. Harrison, Sr.

In chapter one we learned what it means to be created in the image of God, but what does it means to be created in the likeness of God. Genesis 1:26 reads:

> Then God said, "Let us make man ***in our image***, ***after our likeness***. And let them have dominion over the fish of the sea and over the birds of the heavens and over the livestock and over all the earth and over every creeping thing that creeps on the earth." (emphasis added)

In this chapter we hope to enlighten and encourage every man to fulfill his divine destiny of living like God: To think like God, to speak and decree the living Word like God, to subdue and to manage well the things God has entrusted, to be an overcomer and more than a conqueror, and to live a victorious life, a life full of the abundance of God.

There are several major points that need to be examined in this analysis. First, the phrase, "Let ***us*** make in ***our*** image, after ***our*** likeness…" references a plurality of personalities. Second, these personalities agree with the proposed plan. Third, there is an assumption that the reader recognizes image and likeness are not synonyms but imply that image and likeness have two different attributes or traits of God.

So let us examine first start with the definition of a trait or an attribute. Oxford Language Dictionary states that a trait is a distinguishing quality or characteristic, typically one belonging to a person. There is a characteristic and distinguishing quality that God has given to every man, His likeness! This trait is what set us apart from other species He created in the beginning. Man was made in the exact image and likeness of God. We were made to function or operate just like God on the earth. Man was created with the capacity to think, speak, and rule like God on earth.

So, what does it mean to be made in the likeness of God? The term likeness in Hebrew (Strong's Concordance (H 1819 and H 1823) means to compare, by implication, resemblance, concretely, model, and shape. The idea is that mankind is ***like*** God and has similar characteristics to God. However, mankind is not God.

To help our understanding and comprehension of the phrase after our likeness, I want to discuss the similarities between Michael Jordan (MJ), Air Jordan or "His Airness" and Kobe Bryant (KB), the Black Mamba. If you are even a casual fan of the NBA or because of excellent marketing, you have heard of Michael Jordan and Kobe Bryant and how Kobe modeled his game after MJ. The comparisons of Michael and Kobe are striking!

Both Michael and Kobe were gifted athletes and dominated the sport of basketball. Each stood 6' 6" in height, ideal for a shooting guard and both towered over most of their competition. Highly competitive, each possessed an insatiable desire to win, to work, and to lead. Both basketball players played at times with their tongue protruding out of their mouth and used the tongue as a Samurai sword to cut their opponents apart with razor-sharp trash-talking.

Jordan won six NBA titles and Kobe won five. Michael wore two distinct numbers while playing in the NBA – numbers 23 and 45 and so did Kobe – numbers 24 and 8. Michael set the standard for Kobe and Kobe modeled his game to be like Jordans. The similarities in the

way each played the game, how they ran the floor, excelled in defense, the stop-on-a-dime pull-up jump shots over defenders, are uncanny, and it was understood within the NBA ranks and to avid, devoted followers of basketball that Kobe was in every way the heir apparent to Michael. Kobe was born to play basketball and dedicated his life to emulating Michael Jordan.

In 2003 it was reported that after the Washington Wizards defeated the Los Angeles Lakers, MJ told Kobe, who was wearing a pair of Jordan sneakers *"You can wear the shoes, but you can never fill them!"* For the next two weeks after that statement Black Mamba became mute and didn't talk with his teammates and coaches for two weeks. The next time the Lakers played the Wizards, Black Mamba had 55 points and led the Wizards to an easy win.

When we were children, we engaged in fantasy play. In fantasy play we imagine ourselves to be someone else, generally someone with qualities and traits we desire to have our makeup. Children find a character, either a real person or a pretend superhero and attempt to model their attitudes and behavior after that character. No one told us to find a model. We innately sought out those characteristics that attracted us. For Kobe, like so many other young men, it was Michael Jordan. However, most of the time, boys want their hero to be their father.

It is not wrong or unscriptural to desire to be like God. Psalm 139: 13-14 declares:

> *For you formed my inward parts; you knitted me together in my mother's womb. I praise you, for I am fearfully and wonderfully made. Wonderful are your works; my soul knows it very well. And this is supported by Ephesians 2: 10 which tells us, "For we are his workmanship, created in Christ Jesus for good works, which God prepared beforehand, that we should walk in them.*

In this regard Jesus demonstrated the principle of being created to be like God. In 1 John 14: 9: *Jesus said to him, "Have I been with you so long, and you still do not know me, Philip? Whoever has seen me has seen the Father. How can you say, 'Show us the Father?"*

From a genetic viewpoint Genesis 5: 1-3 helps us to understand this phenomenon:

> *This is the book of the generations of Adam. When God created man, He made him in the likeness of God.* **2** *Male and female He created them, and He blessed them and named them Man when they were created. When Adam had lived 130 years, he fathered a son in his own likeness, after his image, and named him Seth.*

It is a common idiom that is used among seasoned Christians, that we have the DNA (deoxyribonucleic acid) of God. God has fruit and His word, which He refers to as seed. God doesn't truly have spiritual DNA (God is a Spirit) but he did create mankind with a set of characteristics and traits that resembled Himself, the fruit of His Spirit. The ability to transfer a set of characteristics was established by God, then recreated or given to Adam, who created a son in his image.

Years ago, I bought a new car for my wife, First Lady Crystal. It was equipped with a vanity license plate that read, "See me, see God!" What a bold statement of our faith, desire, and commitment to God. It was an amazing confession of a believer, that our faith is to live a life that reflects Jesus. It was our desire, my wife and me to live like Jesus Christ, according to Hebrews 1: 3, *"Who being the brightness of his glory, and the express image of his person, and upholding all things by the word of his power, when he had by himself purged our sins, sat down on the right hand of the Majesty on high":*

What was so surprising to us is that this desire, to be like Jesus, was met with some strong criticism from other Christians friends we knew. Soon afterwards, these friends were calling us arrogant, ignorant, and potentially antichrist. Wow! Their attitudes were reflected as a kind questioning relationship, "how dare you equate yourself to be like God" or "So what do you mean by see me see God?" It was unbelievable. Our friends encouraged us to remove the license plate. Their belief or fear was that our confession of faith might cast a shadow, embarrass, or create a negative reflection on the church if we behaved unseeingly with an experience of road rage and behaved in a way that did not reflect God-like characteristics or traits.

What our friends and other members of the church did not understand was that the license plate was an open reminder to us to behave in a way that pleased God. It was an intentional method to reduce or mitigate the aggressive driving style we exhibited from time-to-time. We were not afraid to declare our faith because we were not ashamed of the gospel, the "good news!" because it is the power of salvation. It was a visual reminder of His mercy and grace that was extended to our family. Without His grace we knew we were hopelessly lost. Jesus repeatedly said to the disciples, It is my will to do the will of the Father, or I always do what I see the Father doing. What our friends failed to realize or accept was our personal decision and desire to pattern our lives and raise our family according to Deuteronomy 11: 18-21:

> *You shall therefore lay up these words of mine in your heart and in your soul, and you shall bind them as a sign on your hand, and they shall be as frontlets between your eyes. You shall teach them to your children, talking of them when you are sitting in your house, and when you are walking by the way, and when you lie down, and when you rise. You shall write them on the*

> *doorposts of your house and on your gates, that your days and the days of your children may be multiplied in the land that the LORD swore to your fathers to give them, as long as the heavens are above the earth.*

Another important question to consider, "Why did God create mankind in His likeness?" The answer to this question will put your life on track to fulfill your individual purpose and contribute to the establishment of His kingdom. Though we are not God we are created to be like God. Paul exhorts this message in Romans 8: 14-17 and Galatians 4: 4-7:

> *For all who are led by the Spirit of God are sons of God. For you did not receive the spirit of slavery to fall back into fear, but you have received the Spirit of adoption as sons, by whom we cry, "Abba! Father!"* [16] *The Spirit himself bears witness with our spirit that we are children of God, and if children, then heirs—heirs of God and fellow heirs with Christ, provided we suffer with him in order that we may also be glorified with him. (Romans 8:15)*

> *But when the fullness of time had come, God sent forth his Son, born of woman, born under the law, to redeem those who were under the law, so that we might receive adoption as sons. And because you are sons, God has sent the Spirit of his Son into our hearts, crying, "Abba! Father!" So, you are no longer a slave, but a son, and if a son, then an heir through God. (Galatians 4: 4-7)*

Initially, when we were made in the image and likeness of God mankind or Adam was truly a son of God. However, at the exact moment of Adam's transgression mankind took on a new nature and a different relationship with God. The character of God was separated from man. The traits or fruit of God had been altered and distorted. Sin had now entered the world and into the nature of mankind. Man, who had only experienced the goodness of God, now had to live in a world where sin and evil surrounded him.

Our desire to eagerly fulfill the will of God had suddenly changed. The original plan of God for man to have dominion here on earth was not changed but had been altered. The perfect environment created for mankind, by God's will, wisdom, and work (effort), now required mankind to live by his wits, his intellect, and his work. Men would experience sweat, pain, and fatigue in management of the earth. Women would experience sweat, pain, and fatigue in the management of the family. Mankind would experience deceit, destruction, and death, which was not experienced before sin.

Because of the original sin of Adam, everyone born from Adam was born in sin and has a sin nature. This is the reason Jesus told Nicodemus emphatically, "Truly, truly, I say to you, unless one is born again, he cannot see the kingdom of God." Nicodemus said to him, "How can a man be born when he is old? Can he enter a second time into his mother's womb and be born?" Jesus answered, "Truly, truly, I say to you, unless one is born of water and the Spirit, he cannot enter the kingdom of God. That which is born of the flesh is flesh, and that which is born of the Spirit is spirit.

The need for man to be transformed from flesh to spirit; from sin to righteousness, is found in the story of Jacob. Jacob is the son of Isaac and Rebecca, and he is the twin brother of Esau. We are informed that Jacob's name in Hebrew means heel-catcher, supplanter, one who follows behind, deceiver, and trickster. His name revealed his innate characteristics. Jacob was very cunning and selfish. Throughout his life Jacob plotted and schemed to get the things he wanted through trickery. And just like Adam, who tried to have his needs met without God, Jacob misused his gifts to manipulate others.

All the trickery, the deception, and shenanigans were unnecessary because before Jacob was born, God had a plan and destiny for Jacob that was initially established with Abraham, his grandfather in Genesis 12: 1-3:

> Now the LORD said[a] to Abram, "Go from your country[b] and your kindred and your father's house to the land that I will show you. [2] And I will make of you a great nation, and I will bless you and make your name great, so that you will be a blessing. [3] I will bless those who bless you, and him who dishonors you I will curse, and in you all the families of the earth shall be blessed.

God had established an unbreakable covenant, one that ensured Abraham and his descendants would be blessed. There was no need for Jacob to deceptively plot and plan how to get things. The blessings of God were already determined and predestined by God through His foreknowledge and wisdom. Genesis 17: 1-7 reads:

> *When Abram was ninety-nine years old the LORD appeared to Abram and said to him, "I am God Almighty; walk before me, and be blameless, that I may make my covenant between me and you and may multiply you greatly. "Then Abram fell on his face. And God said to him, "Behold, my covenant is with you, and you shall be the father of a multitude of nations. No longer shall your name be called Abram, but your name shall be Abraham, for I have made you the father of a multitude of nations. I will make you exceedingly fruitful, and I will make you into nations, and kings shall come from you. And I will establish my covenant between me and you and your offspring after you throughout their generations for an everlasting covenant, to be God to you and to your offspring after you.*

If Jacob knew and believed the covenant God established with Abraham, he would have realized that greatness and kingdom authority was the plan of God for his life, his destiny. Moreover, when Rebecca his mother was pregnant with twins Esau and Jacob, the Lord spoke to Rebecca about her pregnancy in Genesis 25: 21-26:

> *And Isaac prayed to the LORD for his wife because she was barren. And the LORD granted his prayer, and Rebekah his wife conceived. The children struggled together within her, and she said, "If it is thus, why is this happening to me?" So she went to inquire of the LORD. And the LORD said to her, "Two nations are in your womb, and two peoples from within you[c] shall be divided the one shall be stronger than the other, the older shall serve the younger." When her days to give birth were completed, behold, there were twins in her womb. The first came out red, all his body like a hairy cloak, so they called his name Esau. Afterward his brother came out with his hand holding Esau's heel, so his name was called Jacob.[d] Isaac was sixty years old when she bore them.*

Man of God, it is important for you to know and believe that God has a plan for you and no matter what you have gone through, what has happened to, or what you have done, the plan may have been altered or distorted, but it has not changed. From his birth Jacob has become a master of deception and trickery. As Jacob grows and develops, however, he falls in love, has children, and begins to have a different perspective on life. Maybe that's you. When you were younger, maybe you were "a wild and crazy guy!" Maybe you were really good at "gaming" or "ghosting" others, and maybe, just maybe you were just a straight-up, old fashion Atomic Dog (bow wow wow, yippie yo, yippie yay!) abusing and using any and everybody! God still has a plan for your life and God has not changed His mind about you.

Given all the dirt and the wrong Jacob did to almost everyone he met it is now surprising that someone retaliated against Jacob. And that someone was his brother Esau, who wanted to kill Jacob. Out fear of Esau and for the safety of his wives, Leah and Rachel, and their family, Jacob sought the Lord. In Genesis 32: 22-28:

> *The same night he arose and took his two wives, his two female servants, and his eleven children, and crossed the ford of the Jabbok. He took them and sent them across the stream, and*

everything else that he had. And Jacob was left alone. And a man wrestled with him until the breaking of the day. When the man saw that he did not prevail against Jacob, he touched his hip socket, and Jacob's hip was put out of joint as he wrestled with him. Then he said, "Let me go, for the day has broken." But Jacob said, "I will not let you go unless you bless me." And he said to him, "What is your name?" And he said, "Jacob." Then he said, "Your name shall no longer be called Jacob, but Israel, for you have striven with God and with men, and have prevailed."

Jacob's name was changed to Israel, to fit his new identity, his new character and the traits that caused him to resemble God. Israel means, "One who prevails, is victorious, a prince." An extension of the meaning of Israel is "One who is ruled by God to rule like God." This is you, man of God, created to be ruled by God to rule like God. To have dominion.

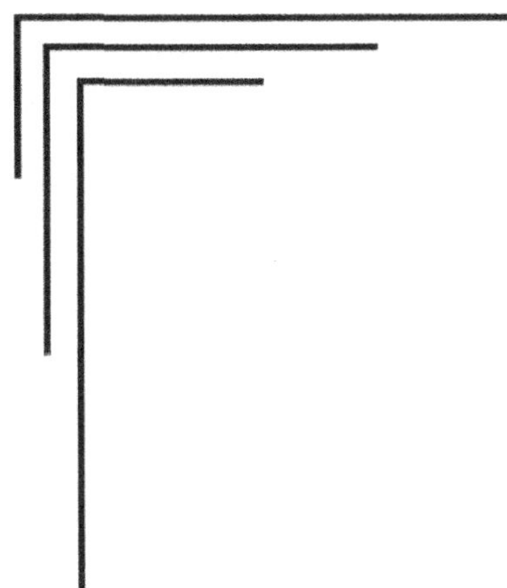

Chapter Three

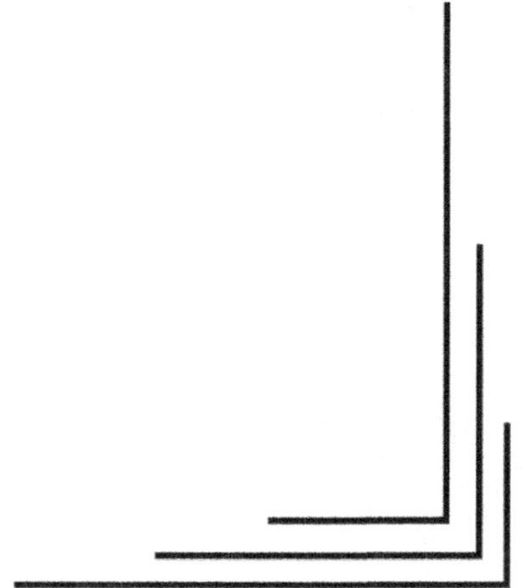

The Dominion and Authority of God

William Morse

It is not uncommon for people to interchangeably use the words dominion and authority. As nouns, the difference between dominion and authority is that dominion is power or the use of power; sovereignty over something; stewardship; supremacy. Authority is the power contained in a status, position, or identity to enforce laws, rules or give commandments (orders). This does not just apply to people or things. The concept of dominion applies to everything in the visible and invisible world when you are a kingdom citizen.

Almost everything people know and the decisions they make come from information they get through their five senses. To be any Godly good, that must change. We can't live our life based on what we see, touch, taste, hear or smell. All those senses fulfill a natural physical and psychological function to help us operate in the natural realm. The fall of man was connected directly to those senses and guess what? Our sins connected to our senses will always lead to death and destruction – The lust of the eye, the lust of the flesh and the pride of life are always *"sin"sational*! Sin is good for a season, but ultimately is doomed for failure.

This approach to living also hides the reality that we all live in one of two kingdoms: The kingdom of light of the kingdom of darkness. And here is the reality that most men don't want to face – you are in control, or you are being controlled by the king of one of those kingdoms. We are not of this world, just as Jesus said in John 17:16. Just as Jesus went to consecrate himself; we must do the same. We were not created or reborn to be dominated by the natural or spiritual realm, but to have dominion and authority over it. We were made in the image and likeness of God, Who declared in Genesis 1: 26-28:

> *Then God said, "Let us make man in our image, after our likeness. And let them have dominion over the fish of the sea and over the birds of the heavens and over the livestock and over all the earth and over every creeping thing that creeps on the earth." So God created man in his own image, in the image of God he created him; male and female he created them. And God blessed them; And God blessed them. And God said to them, "Be fruitful and multiply and fill the earth and subdue it and have dominion over the fish of the sea and over the birds of the heavens and over every living thing that moves on the earth."*

Dominion Requires a Change to Kingdom Thinking

To understand the kingdom of heaven and the dominion authority that the believer has in this kingdom you must change your thinking to kingdom thinking. Natural or carnal thinking are the things you can see, touch, hear, smell and taste. The laws and rules that are understood by man have been revealed to man. Our understanding of these rules and laws gives mankind comfort and a sense of dominion. The principles that govern this world have been learned and taught in institutes of higher learning. However, all these things come from natural learning of a legally limiting system.

Recently, I flew from Baltimore to Chicago and then to Maui, Hawaii. I had one connecting flight, so I was on a Boeing 707 and a Boeing 747. Both planes were filled with passengers to capacity, not an extra seat on either plane. With passengers and cargo included, the maximum take-off weight for the Boeing 707 is 333,600 pounds and the 747 is 606,000 pounds. The gravitational pull from the earth is stronger the heavier the object. So how did those two planes get off the ground and into the sky and fly at 38,000 feet?

Man had to learn the rules and laws of gravity and then establish dominion over those rules. To survive 38,000 feet in the air, man also had to create a new environment within the plane. The pilots who were flying by instrumentation had to learn and then apply new skills. They had to establish communications with air traffic controllers and trust they were being guided to a place that could not see and to a location (spin of the earth) that was constantly moving. All things working together, fitly joined together to ensure a safe flight.

This is analogous to how the kingdom of heaven works and why men must learn how to walk and work the dominion God has created for us. For the citizens of God, we operate in a different domain. 1 Corinthians 2: 9 – 16:

> What is the mind of Christ and how do I change my thinking? Dominion first begins in your mind and is presented as choice. God is and has always been about choice.

Romans 12:2 says it best:

> *And be not conformed to this world: but be ye transformed by the renewing of your mind, that ye may prove what is that good, and acceptable, and perfect will of God."*

Here is a useful way to think about transforming and renewing your mind. I referred to it as F-cubed – Free – Feed - Focus:

- Free your mind
- Feed your mind
- Focus your mind

I heard a pastor speak on this once and I was spiritually awakened. It gave me something I could work with. It gave me something that I could use as a foundation to change my thinking, to change my mind. A renewed mind is a powerful thing.

1. I noticed every negative or wrong thought. When they came, I would write them down, then I would cast them out. With prayer, I would ask the Lord to help free me from them. And I found that when that thought showed up, the Holy Ghost would say, "You don't need to think about that."

2. I would start feeding my mind - I cast out negative thoughts and I would replace those thoughts with scriptures. So, when unwanted thoughts showed up, the Holy Ghost would say, "You don't need to think on that, think on this," and he would give me the scripture.

3. With these things in place, it made it easier to focus on the word of God, focus my mind on good things. Then, I begin to work on only saying things that I wanted out of my mouth. If I didn't want it, I didn't say it. I began to pray for revelation before I read and meditated on the word. I only wanted to know what the Father wanted me to know.

So, every time a crazy thought comes to my mind, I cast it down before it comes out of my mouth. If it did come out of my mouth, I learned how to repent quickly and bind it here on earth and lose the opposite in heaven.

Philippians 4:8-9

> *Finally, brethren, whatsoever things are true, whatsoever things are honest, whatsoever things are just, whatsoever things are pure, whatsoever things are of good report; if there be any virtue, and if there be any praise, think on these things.*

What I have learned is that the word can't be separated from Jesus, so when you read the word, you are reading Jesus to strengthen your spirit with food for the renewing of my mind. When I got saved, that affected my spirit, but my mind still had to be renewed. Before salvation, my mind, body, and spirit were conformed to the worldly way of living. My engine, energy, my body, and mind were all out of alignment. Body and mind are natural, and the spirit is supernatural. When Jesus was raised from the grave, he took care of the supernatural, the spirit, but He left our mind renewal up to us. Our body and mind should be taking orders or instructions from our spirit but the mind a lot of times is not on the same page as our spirit. So, the body goes where the mind says go or do.

The Father didn't create us that way. He created us to be branches of the true vine. The branch gets everything it needs to row from the true vine. When I learned that, I knew I already had the victory of life in life. The doctors had told me that I couldn't and would not work again, but the word says in Psalm 91:3,16:

> *3 – Surely, He shall deliver thee from the snare of the fowler, and from the noisome pestilence.*
>
> *16 – With long life will I satisfy Him and shew Him my salvation.*

So, when cancer came to visit, it was evicted. I would quote Psalm 91:10:

> *There shall no evil befall thee, neither shall any plague come nigh thy dwelling.*

Two months later when my heart was attacked I quoted Psalm 91:13:

> *Thou shalt tread upon the lion and adder: the young lion and dragon shalt thou trample under feet.*

Being a kingdom citizen gives me the right to these promises. The more I study the word, the deeper my relationship gets with the Father. The more promises are revealed. I am trying to be like Jesus because he said we could. John 14:12 tells us:

> *Do also and greater works if I believeth in Him.*

The closer in relationship is with God I get, the clearer the meaning of dominion and authority becomes. Though earth belongs to God, He has given dominion authority to man to manage His affairs on the earth. The enemy will come, and he will go, but always remember he is a defeated foe. We have been given the power to let God's light shine on earth. We, our spirit, are already seated in high places. We oversee establishing the kingdom's atmosphere here on earth. The darkness that's covering the earth, we are to shine our light on it. We are to remember Jesus said, "*...I will give unto thee the keys of the kingdom of heaven...*" Matthew 16:19.

In my walk, I have also seen grace working in my life. For the times when I don't free, feed or focus, God keeps me on the right path. When I step off the path, he pulls me back and lets me see where I have made an error. He will do the same for you.

My prayer for you is found in Matthew 6: 9:

> *Our Father which art in heaven, Hallowed be thy name, thy kingdom come, thy will be done in earth, as it is in heaven. Give us this day our daily bread. And forgive us our debts, as we forgive our debtors. And lead us not into temptation but deliver us from evil. For thine is kingdom, and the power, and the glory, forever Amen.*

William Morse is a proud father of six children, grandfather of 12 children, and great grandfather of 4 children. Brother Morse is an Army veteran of three years, who served during the Vietnam Era. He was honorably discharged with the rank of Sergeant.

Currently, William Morse is a Class A contractor, receiving his license in 1995. He has dedicated his life to building the kingdom of God in the earth and renovating lives with the assistance of the Holy Spirit. Understanding the importance of having godly men in his life, Brother Morse seeks wise counsel from Pastor Edward Clemons and Pastor Jay T. Harrison, Sr.

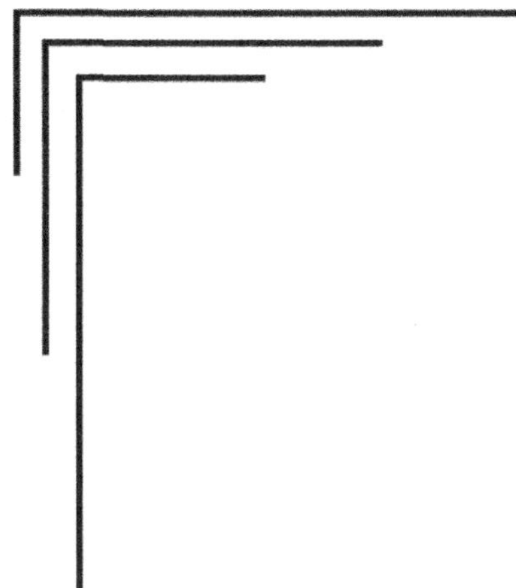

Chapter Four

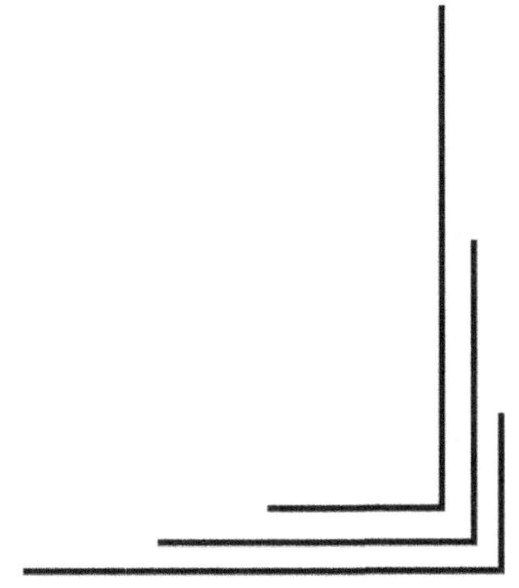

The Blessing of God

Jay T. Harrison, Sr.

September 26, 2022, marked the beginning of a new season for me, and the end of an old one. I became free when I decided to become transparent and share the ugly, gory truth about me. Jesus was absolutely on point when He said, “If you abide in my word, you are truly my disciples, and you will know the truth, and the truth will set you free.” There are some things you wish you could avoid; truths you wish you didn’t have to tell. You know that once you tell it you will have to face shame, guilt, and hurt to self and others. However, you tell painful truths because you know truth transforms.

As a man of God here is the first lesson in understanding the blessing, what it means to a son in the kingdom of God. You are blessed when you receive the unending, everlasting love of our Father. Because in the love of the Father found in the person of Jesus Christ, there is no condemnation, no guilt and shame. However, let me clear, there may be hurt and pain! There are always consequences for behavior, even after you receive His grace and mercy.

King Solomon reminds all of us that there is a time and a season for everything (Ecclesiastes 3: 1- 8):

> *There is a time for everything, and a season for every activity under the heavens: a time to be born and a time to die, a time to plant and a time to uproot, a time to kill and a time to heal, a time to tear down and a time to build, a time to weep and a time to laugh, a time to mourn and a time to dance, a time to scatter stones and a time to gather them, a time to embrace and a time to refrain from embracing, a time to search and a time to give up, a time to keep and a time to throw away, a time to tear and a time to mend, a time to be silent and a time to speak, a time to love and a time to hate, a time for war and a time for peace.*

In my case, it was a time of blessing and a time of disaster. Like Adam, blessed by God with a woman made especially and specifically for him, a perfect complement and helper, I too, fell to temptation, the lust of the eye, the lust of the flesh, and the pride of life. I was unfaithful to God, to my wife and to my family. I thank God every day for His grace, for my wife and family; that we were blessed to survive the ups and downs of that season. Most couples and families do not survive this journey! What was the journey, the time of blessings and a time of disaster? Infidelity.

This journey, for me, began with my covenant vow to God and then when I said to my wife: "For better or worse, for richer and poor, in sickness and health until death do us part!" When these words are recited, few of us think about committing to the worse, the poor, the sickness, until death. The illusion of those wedding vows is that everything is going to be perfect. King Solomon, in the Book of Ecclesiastes, attempts to educate the reader by explaining the polarity of seasons. In every season there will be a period of transition. It is in each season, when things are changing, that you must remain committed and faithful through the process. Remaining committed and faithful,

especially during the changing seasons found in relationships, is ***hard work.***

In the beginning of marital relationships, the courtship and honeymoon season is romantic, sexy, and blissful. However, as seasons change the challenge in relationships is to remain humble in His presence, committed and faithful to your vows, and vulnerable and honest with your spouse. This is not easy, but it's worth fighting for!

I had all but ruined my marriage by trying to fulfill my selfish desires. It was my arrogance and pride that led to my covetous pursuits to gratify my insatiable sexual appetites. God created sex and sexual desire. His divine plan for sex is that it was to be used in the context of a marital relationship. One of the leading causes for divorce in America is marital infidelity, sometimes referred to legally as irretrievable breakdown in the marriage or irreconcilable differences. God calls it what it is, sin!

Well, it's just sex! That's how American society views it; an intimate act between two consenting adults. But in the eyes of God sex outside of marriage is sin! We must renew our minds to the will of God. And it is more than "just sex." It was the type of sin that reflects an attitude that is a direct affront to God. The idea of cheating behavior has become so normalized we believe it is normal, that all men do it! No, it's not normal! It's ab-normal! It is the abuse or abnormal use of something purposely designed by God to be used to secure the intimacy between spouses.

Wait! Some of you who know my pedigree and history might ask, "Aren't you a pastor?" Yes, I am! I am the son of Bishop James L. Harrison; I was out of control! And to make matters worse I was still on the job! Overseer Jay T. Harrison, the well-respected overseer and pastor. The son of a well-respected and incredibly influential bishop and pastor in one of the largest religious denominations in America. Truly, I had it going-on, I had it all.

And at that time, I was also just like David and Samson. Arrogant men who believed they were entitled or deserved everything they desired. I was driven, controlled by my fleshly desires. Interestingly, Jesus was tempted by the same three desires in the wilderness: the lust of the eye, the lust of the flesh, and the pride of life. However, Jesus was driven and controlled by the Spirit (Luke 4: 1-2):

> *And Jesus being full of the Holy Ghost returned from Jordan, and was led by the Spirit into the wilderness, being forty days tempted of the devil. And in those days, he did eat nothing: and when they were ended, he afterward hungered.*

In both cases, David and Samson knew they desired things they should not have. When King David should have been at war, it only took one look out his window for David to become distracted and what he saw messed him up! Samson had similar challenges; always wanting what he ought not have. These anointed men, like me, were on the job! We all were distracted by our position, power, and rapacious appetite for sex.

David, Samson, and Jay, all believed it was okay to chase after the forbidden low-hanging fruit because it is easy to get, but nevertheless, off limits. For brief moments, the attitude was, not to do His will, but to get whatever we wanted! In those moments God's words and commandments concerning sin; to flee from sin and pursue the kingdom of God and His righteousness are God's standard for kingdom living were not important. How can you forget or ignore the love of God and the beauty of holiness?

By now most have heard about the troubles of Ime Udoka, former head coach of the Boston Celtics. Udoka was suspended for one year after it was discovered, within the Boston Celtics organization, that he was in a consensual sexual relationship with a female, subordinate staffer. Though consensual, this behavior was in direct violation with organizational ethics and policy. Furthermore, Ime Udoka has been engaged to Nia Long since 2015 and together they have an eleven-year-old son.

I'm citing this story because it supports my belief that you can have everything; a great job, successful career, popular status (position, power, and popularity), and in his case a fiancée and child, and in a moment, lose it all. You lose it all by being incredibly selfish, by believing you can do anything and get away with it, and that you are beyond the watchful eyes of a Holy God.

One day I was sitting alone in my office. I didn't think much of it at the time when in walked this single female, a member of our ministry team. Like King David, who gazed at the wife of Uriah and wanted her, the seed and sin of infidelity was planted in me. Let me clear, sin begins in your mind and heart before it becomes an action. The longer you entertain the thoughts contrary to God's righteousness the closer you are to committing the sin. In Matthew 5: 28 Jesus clearly makes this point:

> *But I say to you that whoever looks at a woman to lust for her has already committed adultery with her in his heart.*

Suddenly, what I had secretly been thinking had now become the primary focus of my desire. This is from the blessed position as a pastor and overseer. I was a happily married man of twenty-four years and father of eight children. I was an anointed man of God, with positional power and authority, surrounded by family and friends from around the world.

Right away I knew I was wrong. Immediately, I was captured

by guilt and shame. Instead of running to God I ran from Him. I ran from His voice and hid. How does one hide from God? I stopped seeking God in intimate prayer. My worship became empty. Having grown up in church and because I was the director of intercessory prayer I knew how to through the motions and traditions of worship. I read the bible to find sermons, not to know Him. I tried to cover up my fall by acting as if nothing happened.

I lived a life of duplicity, being religious and rebellious at the same time. My attempts to hide sin, the guilt and shame only made it worse. I struggled in this deceptive and deceitful relationship with God, my wife and family, and my church congregation while I was actively involved in an adulterous relationship for three years. I felt just like Apostle Paul, who wrote this honest confession in Romans chapter 7: 19-25:

> *For I know that good itself does not dwell in me, that is, in my sinful nature. For I have the desire to do what is good, but I cannot carry it out. For I do not do the good I want to do, but the evil I do not want to do—this I keep on doing. Now if I do what I do not want to do, it is no longer I who does it, but it is sin living in me that does it. So, I find this law at work: Although I want to do good, evil is right there with me. For in my inner being I delight in God's law; but I see another law at work in me, waging war against the law of my mind and making me a prisoner of the law of sin at work within me. What a wretched man I am! Who will rescue me from this body that is subject to death? Thanks be to God, who delivers me through Jesus Christ our Lord! So then, in my mind I am a slave to God's law, but in my sinful nature a slave to the law of sin.*

What happened in my life and how I let it happen are the essential questions that must be asked and answered. James Collins affirms in his book, *Good to Great: Why Some Companies Make the Leap…and Others Don't,* "Good is the enemy of great. And that is one of the key reasons why we have so little that becomes great. Few people attain great lives, in large part because it is just so easy to settle for a good life." That's what happened to Samson, to David and to me, we settled and got too comfortable.

It was the very blessing that God placed in me where I became incarcerated in comfort. God attempted to warn me of the dangers of comfort and complacency. He attempted to provide a way of escape. I heard God telling me no, but I refused to listen to Him. In fact, I told

God to hush, and I turned the volume down on His voice so I could listen to my own. I turned down the volume on God's voice and listened to my own voice in my heart. I became more interested in having what was forbidden, off limits. I concentrated on what I could not have instead of focusing my attention on all the blessings God provided.

When I was told no, I transitioned from a submitted servant and son into *hunt mode,* a hunter of flesh. I had a new God-less purpose; to prove to myself that I still got it! The old man, who I was to kill daily, was revived. My ego began talking to me, massaging my pride, reminding me of past conquests, and leading me, not through the paths of righteousness for His name's sake, but through the paths of death and destruction.

When you're not listening and connected to God, listening to your ego will cause you to fall. I spent at least six years entangled in an affair I knew was wrong and at times I tried to walk away. My heart became so desperate and wicked that nothing else mattered. Now I'm controlled by my flesh. I was no longer living and walking by faith and His Spirit. And so, the flow of the blessing was interrupted, suspended by my stupidity.

The blessing is an empowerment, an endorsement, and an enrichment of the power of God, to help you fulfill the plan of God. The blessing offers you the protection of God that is secured with the promises of God. Apostle Paul writes in the letter to the Church in Rome[1], "For God's gifts and his call can never be withdrawn." The blessing is on you, in you, and with you anywhere, everywhere, and always! Confessing the truth of the word of God, will make us free from the deceitfulness of darkness.

Once exposed I was more afraid of and concerned about how people would see me rather than the damage I created and the people I had hurt. Through disobedience I opened the door to curses. Because I refused to repent from this mindset it was hard to recover and heal. Shame,

---

[1] Romans 11:29 New Living Translation.

selfishness, and seclusion will keep you sin-sick. Although the adulterous relationship ended after three years I remained sin-sick for an additional three years. The memories haunted my heart and filled my mind with insecurities. There was no way God could ever love me again! I so identified with the heart of David in Psalm 51:

> *Have mercy on me, O God, according to your unfailing love; according to your great compassion blot out my transgressions. Wash away all my iniquity and cleanse me from my sin. For I know my transgressions and my sin is always before me. Against you, you only, have I sinned and done what is evil in your sight; so you are right in your verdict and justified when you judge. Surely, I was sinful at birth, sinful from the time my mother conceived me. Yet you desired faithfulness even in the womb; you taught me wisdom in that secret place. Cleanse me with hyssop, and I will be clean; wash me, and I will be whiter than snow. Let me hear joy and gladness; let the bones you have crushed rejoice. Hide your face from my sins and blot out all my iniquity.*

I remember going away to a prayer conference and crying out to God for help. I desperately asked Him, I begged Him to have mercy on me, to deliver me from this sin, this addiction to pride, perversion, and power and restore my relationship, my walk with Him. If the cost was to lose everything to be free, I was willing to lose everything. I wanted to be free. See, my biggest challenge was trying to keep my fall a secret and just go on like nothing ever happened. But that was a big lie and not true repentance. So, I prayed to the Lord whatever it takes, I don't want to lose my relationship with you! Please save me from me was my cry. God heard my cry and saved and restored me.

So, through this journey, what have I learned about the blessings of God? Here are some of the lessons learned:

1. That the love of God is amazing and everlasting.
2. That my sin and your sin is not larger than His grace.
3. That in Jesus Christ, there is no shame and condemnation.

4. That the gifts and calling of God are irrevocable.

However, I learned something about the blessing of God, in Genesis, that had not been clearly revealed to me in my life. In Genesis 1: 28 read carefully:

> ***God blessed them and said to them****, "Be fruitful and increase in number; fill the earth and subdue it. Rule over the fish in the sea and the birds in the sky and over every living creature that moves on the ground."*

God blessed both the man and the woman, the husband and the wife, the father, and the mother. In the New Living Translation, Proverbs 18: 22-24 informs the reader:

> *The man who finds a wife finds a treasure, and he receives favor from the LORD.*

My wife is my treasure, my blessing. I am so blessed and grateful that I'm married to a godly woman. In her I experience the favor of the Lord.

Is she perfect, no! But she is the manifestation of the righteousness and forgiveness of God that can only be found in Jesus Christ. Undoubtedly, my story would have a different ending without the strength and support she provided for me, our family, and for the church. It was her steadfast belief in God and her commitment to our covenant held us together. The greatest challenge in our relationship will be trust! I have learned to trust God with my whole heart. Moreover, I have witnessed firsthand, my wife demonstrates forgiveness and the diligence to do God's will.

To God and my wife, I am forever grateful. Pastor Marvin Sapp said it best, "Never would have made it, Never could have made it, without You. I would have lost it all, but now I see how You were there for me. I never would have made it without You. That is so true! We are still standing, stronger, wiser, better, so much better! And blessed!

Overseer Jay T. Harrison Sr. was born at Sacred Heart Hospital on May 25, 1968, and raised in Chester, Pennsylvania. He is the fourth of six children and the only son of the late Bishop James and Pastor Emeritus Lessie Harrison. Pastor Harrison, who was born into a ministry led family, was exposed early on with a rearing that stressed community service. Overseer Harrison is very close to his family and enjoys spending quality time with them.

Mr. Harrison has been married to his wonderful wife and the mother of his children Elder Crystal Harrison for twenty-six years. God has blessed them with eight children: Jay Timothy. Jr., Juanita, Jessika, Katyce Jones, Robert, Romesha, Micah, Mekhi and Seven grandchildren; Jeremiah, Jordan, Aden Isaiah, Jaziah, Dorae and Joy.

Education is highly valued in the Harrison household, with both parents holding advanced degrees. Overseer Harrison attended private Christian schools throughout his academic career, graduating from St. James High School for Boys. Upon graduation, Overseer Harrison attended the Delaware County Institute of Training to become a Nurse's Assistant, where he graduated at the top of his class with honors. Upon relocating to Williamsburg, VA, he became employed by the Eastern State Hospital. After four years of service, a work-related injury caused him to retire. Upon retirement Overseer Harrison increased his involvement in the ministry while at New Life Family Church, serving as the Youth Pastor, a position which prepared him for God's next assignment.

Overseer Harrison was subsequently employed at the Richard Milburn School, which was an alternative educational facility for at-promise youth. The success of that position resulted in Pastor Harrison's promotion to the Williamsburg Department of Social Services working with "At Promise Youth." What began as a Prevention Coordinator ultimately advanced to the Community Services Director during His employment with the Williamsburg James City County Community Action Agency.

Overseer Harrison's passion for community activism extended beyond his employment. He became actively involved in the local NAACP and founded the Williamsburg Community Development Organization, which grew to more than twenty members. Overseer Harrison was also actively involved in the Youth Services Coalition where he served as Chairman of the Safe and Drug Free Schools Dropout Prevention Program, and co-founder of the Neighborhood Basketball League, which continues to serve students in the Williamsburg-James City County, York County, and surrounding localities.

In November of 1999, Rev. Jay T. Harrison Sr. was elected as the first African American Republican and only the second African American to serve on the Board of Supervisors of James City County VA. During his tenure in office Overseer Harrison served as President of the James City County Transit Company, Chairman and Vice-Chairman of the JCSA, Chairman and Vice-Chairman of the James City County Board of Supervisors and the Regional Issues Committee, and two terms as Chairmen of the Greater Hampton Roads Workforce Development Board.

Overseer Harrison's ministerial experience began via his active involvement with his parent's ministry while growing up. Pastor Harrison has served as a Youth Pastor at New Life Family Church located in Williamsburg, Virginia and was the founding Pastor of Living Word Mission. Also having served as the Youth Pastor at Green Springs Chapel he subsequently served as an Elder at Resurrection House International Ministries, and successively founded Keys for Change Family Life Ministries.

Upon his return to Chester, PA he served as Co-Pastor of the True Vine Missionary Full Gospel Baptist Church (MFGBC) under the leadership of his mother, the Rev. Lessie L. Harrison since 2004. He has also founded the Keys For Change Community Development Corporation, the purpose of which is to develop families into strong "Kingdom Citizens" by offering a Marriage Enrichment Ministry, Leadership Training, and the "5 Days of Grace" Healing and Deliverance Crusade.

Overseer Harrison is actively involved in the Full Gospel Baptist Church Fellowship where he currently serves as the State Director of Intercessory Prayer for the region. Overseer Harrison was elevated to the position of Eastern District Overseer for the State of Pennsylvania where he oversees several churches. Overseer Harrison is the founder of Churches United for Harvest. The Keys for Change Sons & Daughters Ministerial Alliance was recently established to provide covering, mentorship and accountability for the licensed and ordained clergy birthed into a ministry leadership role and for those that call him their spiritual father.

True Vine MFGB Church has re-established its weekly bible studies in Philadelphia PA, New Castle Delaware, Penns Grove New Jersey. In 2012 Overseer released the vision for "Clear Direction Ministries" located in Williamsburg, Virginia under the leadership of his spiritual son and daughter Elder Alexander and Elder Elizabeth Butler.

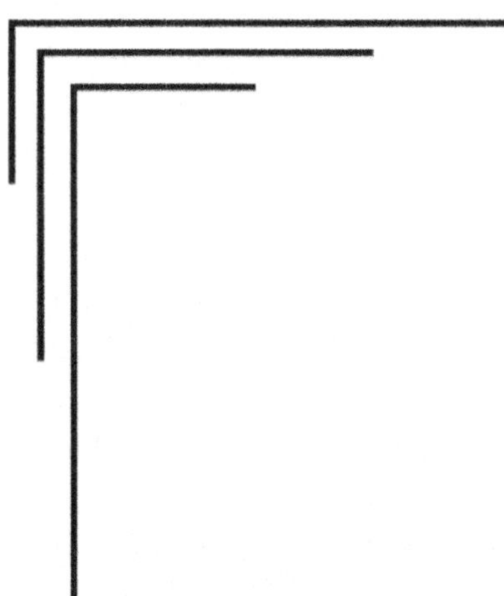

Chapter Five

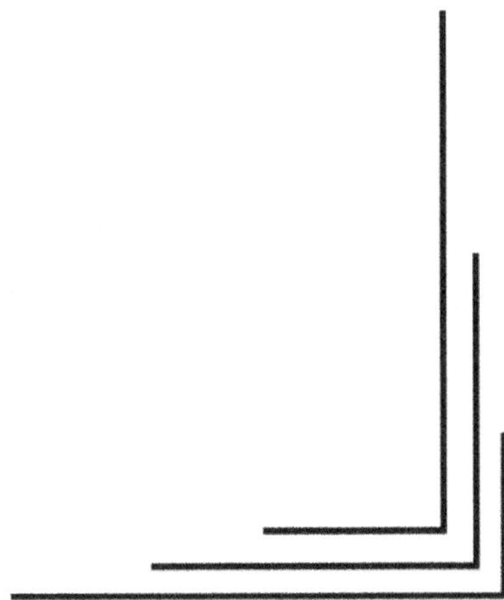

The Faith of God

Alexander Butler

The most important power we possess on earth is our faith in God. It is the chief currency in the kingdom of God. For in it the righteousness of God is revealed from faith to faith; as it is written, the just shall live by faith" (Romans 1:17, NKJV).

Why is it so imperative that we live by faith? I've come to realize that faith is the only thing that threatens the devil and if you have that he cannot succeed. Ephesians 6:11;16 (NKJV) says,

> *Put on the whole armor of God, that you may be able to stand against the wiles of the devil. Above all, taking the shield of faith with which, you will be able to quench all the fiery darts of the wicked one".* Faith is described as a shield that protects the believer from the fiery darts of the enemy. *"So then faith comes*

> *by hearing and hearing by the word of God"* (Romans 10:17 NKJV).
>
> *The grass withers, the flower fades, but the word of God stands forever"* (Isaiah 40:8 NKJV).

It's not by coincidence that the word of God encourages us to walk by faith and not by sight. Hebrews 11:6 says:

> *But without faith it is impossible to please Him, for he who comes to God must believe that He is, and that He is a rewarder of those who diligently seek Him.*

God will always reward unwavering faith. Throughout the remainder of this chapter, you will discover miracles that were conceived in the womb of faith of Jesus Christ. Your faith, man of God, is the driving force that direct you toward your miracle. Together let's arise and fight the good fight of faith according to the word of God.

THE BEGINNING OF FAITH

Hear the Word

So then faith comes by hearing and hearing by the word of God
(Romans 10:17)

Obviously, the prerequisite for faith to grow is to position yourself to hear the word of God. Submit to sound biblical teaching and doctrine that will challenge your faith to develop and grow. Be willing to silence the voice of any and everything that refuses to speak the word of God into your life. Remember, our adversary the devil is always on the prowl looking for whom he may devour. *"The sower sows the word. And these are the ones by the wayside where the word is sown. When they hear, Satan comes immediately and takes away the word that was sown in their hearts"* (Mark 4:14-15 NKJV). Guard your heart by any means necessary.

Believe the Word

Jesus told His disciples to have faith in God. It was the God kind of faith that had the ability to believe in the impossible. Have you ever heard the phrase don't always believe what you hear? Well, when it comes to the word of God you can't believe God until you hear God. Hence faith comes by hearing and hearing by the word of God. Mark 11:23-24: says,

> *For assuredly, I say to you, whoever says to this mountain, Be removed and be cast into the sea, and does not doubt in his heart, but believes that those things he says will be done, he will have whatever he says. Therefore, I say to you, whatever things you ask when you pray, believe that you will receive them, and you will have them.*

Jesus often used an exaggerated statement to make a powerful point. The use of a simile is a literary tool used for making comparisons or illustrating similarities and was not meant to be taken literally. No man can move a real mountain, but the mountain-like obstacles in your life can be removed by faith. For nothing is impossible to those that believe.

The word of God according to (Hebrews 10:23 NKJV) says,

> *Let us hold fast the profession of our faith without wavering; for he is faithful that promised.*

It's a beautiful thing to know that regardless of our imperfections and disobedience towards God and His word, He remains faithful towards us. God will never change or alter His love concerning you. No matter the circumstances or situations, God knows what we need, even when life throws us an unexpected curve ball that challenges your faith.

On May 22, 2017, life threw a curve ball that directly confronted my faith. I received news that significantly challenged and changed the life trajectory of my family. The testing of our faith and what we really believed about God came knocking at our door.

As a believer and faithful follower of Christ, a believer who has been redeemed by the blood of the Lamb; this life-changing curve ball posed a question to me:

> *What do you do when you are face-to-face with a death-like experience?*

How does a man respond when his seventeen-year-old son is given a five-percent chance of survival after experiencing a Traumatic Brain Injury (TBI) due to an unfortunate car accident? To be honest I didn't know how to respond.

The moment will forever be embedded in my mind. On May 22, 2017, a young girl who was a classmate of my son and our neighbor gave me a message that no parent could ever prepare themselves to receive. With tears running down her cheeks, trying to speak through uncontrollably sobbing and her emotional pain, I heard her cracked voice say those words:

> *Juan was in a car accident as he was riding home with a friend and the car flipped over landing upside down. The cops are there but they are not letting*
> *anyone on the scene.*

In that very moment everything I thought I knew about faith and what it meant to believe and trust God was immediately overtaken by the spirit of fear.

Fear has a unique way of gripping you when you least expect it. It comes like a thief in the night looking to steal, kill and destroy. The purpose of fear is that you will succumb to the pain, pressure, and anxiety of the unknown. In that moment fear had a deafening voice. The voice of fear was louder and stronger than my faith, telling me that my son was dead. And if he wasn't dead his life would never be the same.

Until further information was released concerning my son, I had no other choice, at that moment, than to simply trust God and hope for the best. Though God always gives us choice I felt I did not have another alternative. This type of faith was planted early in my life.

After receiving this devastating news, I immediately called my wife, who was working at the time, and told her what had happened. From her belly, where our son was conceived and developed, where he was loved and protected, there was an eruption, like an active volcano, a great scream of agony, despair, and a sense of helplessness.

We immediately rushed to the scene of the accident and from a distance we could see the car was completely upside down. But there was no sign of our son. Instantly, we realized the situation at hand was far worse than what we previously expected. The first responders and police officers immediately held us back and explained to us that our son had already been sent to the local hospital. They further informed us what they believe happened and what possibly caused the accident. We learned our son was a passenger riding with a friend as they were leaving school.

On that day it had rained extremely hard for an extended period. As they were leaving the parking lot his friend was speeding, hit a water spot on the road, and began to hydroplane. The driver apparently lost control of the car resulting in the car flipping over. The driver was able to walk away with a few minor scratches, but our son Juan, who at the time was not wearing his seat belt, was ejected through the sunroof of the car. The Emergency Medical Responders (EMR) thought our son was dead at the scene of the accident, believing the car literally landed on top of Juan.

Thankfully, he was still alive and breathing on his own when they rushed him to the hospital. My wife and I proceeded to our local hospital only to be greeted by numerous
doctors and nurses that led us to a private room. Right away we thought the worst. They explained that our son had experienced intense bleeding, damage and swelling to the head that was beyond their ability to perform an emergency operation. Therefore, they had to send him 45 minutes away to the Medical College of Virginia (MCV) located in Richmond, VA. MCV is one of the top hospitals in the state of Virginia.

Without hesitation we rushed to MCV. We still had no clear knowledge of the severity of the injury. It was not until we arrived at the hospital that we realized our faith in God was about to be tried and tested at a new level.

According to one of the doctors at the MCV Head Trauma Unit, he explained to me and my wife that all head trauma victims that arrive in the (ER) Emergency Room are rated on a scale from 3 to 15. Fifteen means that they are okay to operate. If a patient receives a score between five and three, they normally consider that person dead on arrival. Medical interventions are withheld because of the low probability of success. The trauma specialist explained to us that since our son had just experienced a Traumatic Brain Injury, he was considered a two. Juan was not even on the scale to be considered to have surgery.

Once again, glory be to God, as the doctor spoke these words,

> *Since your son was young, strong, and healthy and he came in with a strong heartbeat and breathing on his*
> *I proceeded to perform the surgery anyway without your consent. The operation to release the pressure and bleeding off the brain was a success and now he is recovering. Would you like to go and see him?*

WE had experienced a miracle! With tears of joy and relief welling in the eyes of my wife we were simply relieved that our son was still alive.

From that very moment, we would begin a 64-day journey of basically living in the hospital as our son was now on the road to recovery.

After only a few days in the Intensive Care Unit (ICU) our faith in God was once again about to be challenged like we have never experienced. It is difficult to imagine the uncertainty and fear that constantly tried to convince us that our son was not going to recover. Fear and doubt can be relentless. Every day the doctors and nurses gave us a grim report that nothing was changing because of his lack of movement and his inability to respond to certain medications.

Basically, all hope was lost and there was nothing else the doctors could do for our son. Now the instructions to my wife and me was that we needed to decide to pull the plug. They proceeded to explain that our son only had a 5% chance of living and if he did live it was a 100% guarantee that he would be a vegetable from the neck down.

> *What do you do when you are face-to-face with a death-like experience?*

In that very moment, my heart was overloaded with uncertainty, hopelessness, pain, hurt, sadness, and the reality that we must decide to terminate the life of our child. I was lost for words and direction. I didn't really know how to make such a life-or-death decision.

My wife and I decided we were willing to oppose the odds and trust God. Then without hesitation, where once there was despair, agony, and a sense of helplessness, my wife, with all boldness and authority, looked directly at the doctor and said:

> *Doctor, with all due respect, I hear what you are saying, and my husband and I appreciate all that you have done for our son. But we will not pull the plug just yet. We have faith and trust in God that He has the final say so concerning our son.*

And as they normally say, the rest is history! After 64 days in the hospital, after numerous head surgeries, constant therapy, and rehabilitation, our son recovered. Juan had to relearn how to walk, talk and eat again. The Medical College of Virginia has labeled Juan, whose name in Hebrew means "gift from God" as the one in a million-miracle son.

Individuals who have experienced traumatic brain injuries like Juan's normally die. If they do live, the individual is placed in a coma induced persistent vegetative state, with limited or no quality of life. Our son's story is still being written to this very day.

After this experience we can truly testify what it means to have faith in God. Through this journey I have learned that faith is action which means it requires us to do something - ***BELIEVE***. It is the grace and mercies of God that sustained my wife and me. You may have a question:

What if our son hadn't lived, would your faith be so strong?

That is a great question. I honestly don't know the answer. However, I do know the God of the mountain is also the God of the valley. He will see you through. Therefore, be encouraged my brother, it doesn't matter what situation you may find yourself in God is able to deliver you.

You very well may be incarcerated, sick in your body, addicted to drugs or fighting for the custody of your child. Just remember that all things work together for good to those who love God, to those who are called according to His purpose. The blessing of God, His purpose is in your life. When you are face-to-face with a life changing situation or a death like experience, simply remind the enemy that no matter what happens, you refuse to pull the plug. Have faith in God, my brother, that you are the candidate for a one in a million miracle:

> *Now to Him who is able to do exceedingly abundantly above all that we ask or think, according to the power that works in us"* (Ephesians 3:20).

God Bless you Man of God

Pastor Alexander Butler, a spiritual son of Overseer Jay T. Harrison, has devoted his life to proclaiming the word of God with simplicity and understanding through the power of the Holy Spirit. Pastor Butler has been active in ministry for over 18 years. He flows in an apostolic-prophetic anointing where he teaches and preaches the rhema word of God that provides direction, healing, and deliverance for the body of Christ.

His vision is to establish a global sound for the kingdom of God through prophecy and revelation, to empower believers for the work of ministry and to engage authentic relationships through networking to advance the will of God according to Ephesians 4: 11-13:

> *And he gave some, apostles; and some, prophets; and some, evangelists; and some, pastors and teachers;*
>
> *For the perfecting of the saints, for the work of the ministry, for the edifying of the body of Christ: Till we all come in the unity of*

> *the faith, and of the knowledge of the Son of God, unto a perfect man, unto the measure of the stature of the fulness of Christ:*

His mission is to teach, transform, train and transition believers to fulfill their God given assignment.

Pastor Butler has been married for 18 years to Elizabeth Butler and together they have four children Caleb, Gabrielle, Juan and Avanda. They currently reside in New Kent, Virginia.

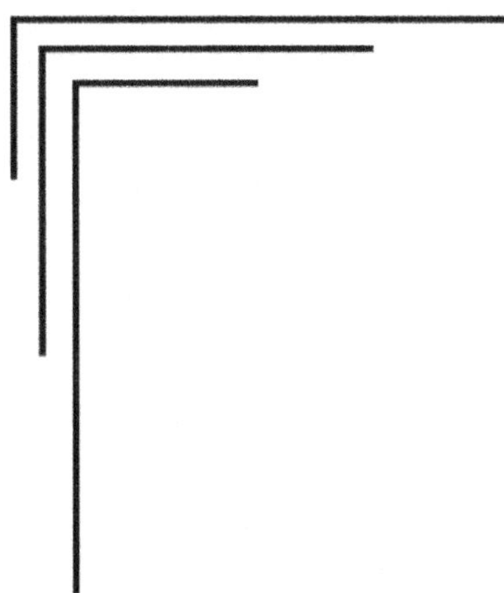

Chapter Six

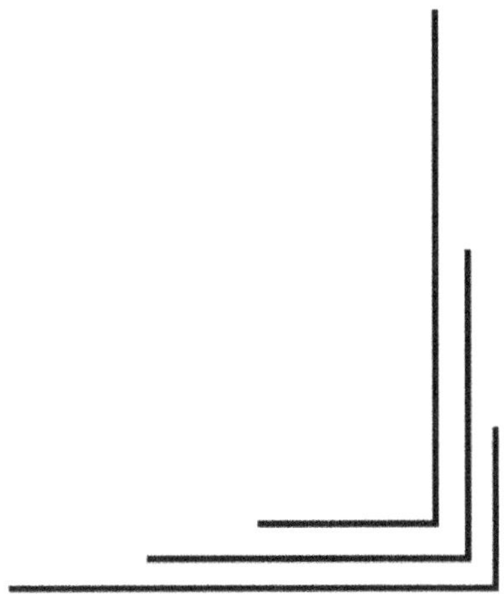

Prayer

Les Parker

One of the most important traits of a man of God is his relationship with God, established in and through prayer. Prayer in its simplest form is communication with God. And, as with all relationships, our relationship with God is strengthened through frequent communication. The more a man prays the stronger his connection is with God. This connection with God is based on three principles:

1. First, a man must believe that God exists (Hebrew 11:6).
2. Second, a man must know that God wants to be in relationship with us.
3. Third, a man must understand all strong relationships are built on communication. This means not only talking to God but listening from God as well.

And what are the key characteristics of a praying man?

a) He studies the Bible so his Prayers agree with God's Word, and studying the Bible is a key piece of that.
b) He knows how to pray his way through the storms in his life. "Stormology" or the storms of life teach us that there are three types of storms in all our lives:

    i. the storm we've just come through
    ii. the storm we're in
    iii. the storm to come.

c) A praying man thanks God for deliverance from the storm he's just come through, praises God with conviction for the victory over the storm he's in and gives thanks for God's strong right hand that will strengthen him for the battle of the storms to come.
d) The fruit of his strong prayer life gives observable evidence of his connection to the vine.

Webster's Dictionary defines the word importune as to press or urge with troublesome persistence. An example of an importune pray-er is found in a parable of exquisite simplicity. You see, our Lord taught not simply that men ought to pray, but that men ought to pray with full heartiness, and press the matter with vigorous energy and brave hearts.

Like 18:1-8 teaches us of persistent prayer in a parable:

> *And he spake a parable unto them to this end, that men ought always to pray, and not to faint; Saying, There was in a city a judge, which feared not God, neither regarded man: And there was a widow in that city; and she came unto him, saying, Avenge me of mine adversary. And he would not for a while: but afterward he said within himself, Though I fear not God, nor regard man; Yet because this widow troubleth me, I will avenge her, lest by her continual coming she weary me. And the Lord said, Hear what the unjust judge saith. And shall not God avenge*

> *his own elect, which cry day and night unto him, though he bears long with them? I tell you that he will avenge them speedily. Nevertheless, when the Son of man cometh, shall he find faith on the earth?*

The poor woman's case was a most hopeless one, but her importunity, her undaunted persistence brings hope from the realms of despair and creates success where neither success nor its conditions existed. There could be no stronger case, to show how unwearied and dauntless importunity gains its ends where everything else fails. The preface to this parable says: "He spake a parable to this end, that men ought always to pray and not to faint." He knew that men would soon get faint-hearted in praying, so to hearten us, that is to give us confidence, God gives this picture of the marvelous power of importunity.

Christ puts importunity as a distinguishing characteristic of a true praying man. We must not only pray, but we must also pray with great urgency, with intentness, and intensity, and with repetition. We must not only pray, but we must pray again and again. We must not get tired of praying. Jesus Christ made it very plain that the secret of prayer and its success lie in our urgency to God's will. This urgency is not rooted in our own strength or belief in our abilities

We must press our prayers upon God because of our total belief in the sovereign power of God. It's this urgency of prayer that gives undisputed evidence of a man's faith in and reliance on God as his deliverer and his strength. In fact, the first lessons of importunity are taught in Matthew 7:7-8:

> *Ask, and it shall be given you; seek, and ye shall find; knock, and it shall be opened unto you: For every one that asketh receiveth; and he that seeketh findeth; and to him that knocketh it shall be opened.*

A praying man knows with an unshakable faith that it is prayer which allows him to advance in his relationship with God.

The trait of a God-fearing praying man is the evidence, or fruit, of his walk with and connection to God. He's humble and submitted to the will of God, yet bold in the expression of his faith. He deals with the same storms which we all do, yet though his flesh be troubled his spirit is at peace.

Furthermore, the trait of a praying man is not just subjective, or internal, but objective and observable. His spirit or inner man gives evidence of his relationship with God, strengthened through prayer, with his Father. It's this fruit of the Spirit that gives that observable evidence of his connection with God.

A praying man is a confident man for he knows who he is and whose he is (who he belongs to). Praying men have influence with God, of whom God commits Himself and His Gospel. Praying men are men who allow the Holy Spirit to make intercession for them. Holy Spirit and Prayer go hand in hand.

Men who pray may have their own opinions, goals, and desires; but they are willing to set those down when it is a matter of obedience to the Lord. Praying men pray according to the instructs of Jesus, found in Matthew 6: 9-13:

> *After this manner therefore pray ye: Our Father which art in heaven, Hallowed be thy name. Thy kingdom come, Thy will be done in earth, as it is in heaven. Give us this day our daily bread. And forgive us our debts, as we forgive our debtors. And lead us not into temptation but deliver us from evil: For thine is the kingdom, and the power, and the glory, forever. Amen.*

Praying men are warriors and warriors are men humble before God and remain humble in the presence of other men. They recognize there is no need to be arrogant or self-righteous. They are consistently putting God's will and the well-being of others above their own desires.

As we enter the new year, 2023, our nation and our world is crying desperately for men who know how to pray, who are in relationship with

God and with other men. In increasing numbers, the men who are so greatly needed in this age are those who have learned the business of praying. These brothers have learned strength is found when on their knees. David conveys this message in his Psalm 27: 1-14:

> *The LORD is my light and my salvation; whom shall I fear? the LORD is the strength of my life; of whom shall I be afraid? When the wicked, even mine enemies and my foes, came upon me to eat up my flesh, they stumbled and fell. Though a host should encamp against me, my heart shall not fear though war should rise against me, in this will I be confident.*
>
> *One thing have I desired of the LORD, that will I seek after; that I may dwell in the house of the LORD all the days of my life, to behold the beauty of the LORD, and to enquire in his temple. For in the time of trouble he shall hide me in his pavilion: in the secret of his tabernacle shall he hide me; he shall set me up upon a rock.*
>
> *And now shall mine head be lifted up above mine enemies round about me: therefore, will I offer in his tabernacle sacrifices of joy; I will sing, yea, I will sing praises unto the LORD. Hear, O LORD, when I cry with my voice: have mercy also upon me, and answer me. When thou saidst, Seek ye my face; my heart said unto thee, Thy face, LORD, will I seek.*
>
> *Hide not thy face far from me; put not thy servant away in anger: thou hast been my help; leave me not, neither forsake me, O God of my salvation. When my father and my mother forsake me, then the LORD will take me up.*
>
> *Teach me thy way, O LORD, and lead me in a plain path, because of my enemies. Deliver me not over unto the will of mine enemies: for false witnesses are risen up against me, and such as breathe out cruelty. I had fainted, unless I had believed to see the goodness of the LORD in the land of the living.*

Wait on the LORD: be of good courage, and he shall strengthen thine heart: wait, I say, on the LORD.

Deacon Leslie Parker, Sr. is a loved husband of one wife and the proud father of five children. He also has three grandchildren. Deacon Parker is an honorably discharged veteran of the U.S. Navy, having served during the Vietnam Era. Brother Parker was ordained to the office of deacon in October 2015. He presently serves as the Chairman of Deacon Ministry at King of Kings Baptist Ministries, Bishop Lee C. Carter, Pastor and State Bishop of Pennsylvania, Full Gospel Baptist Church Fellowship.

Leslie Parker holds a business degree as a paralegal specialist. He recently retired in 2022 from the Allegheny County, Pennsylvania Department of Court Records. Currently, Mr. Parker is the President/CEO, Parker House Investors, Inc.

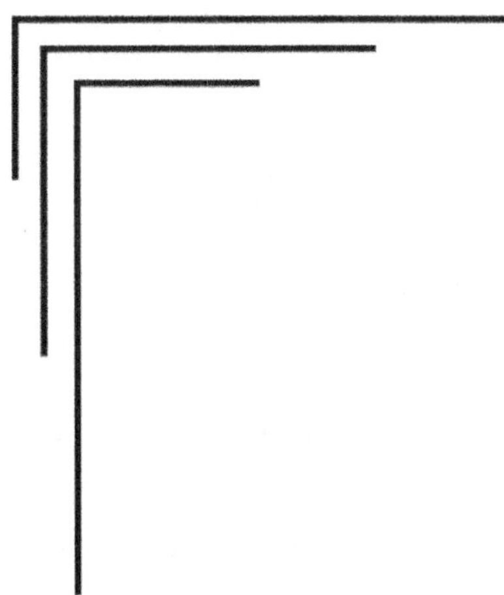

Chapter Seven

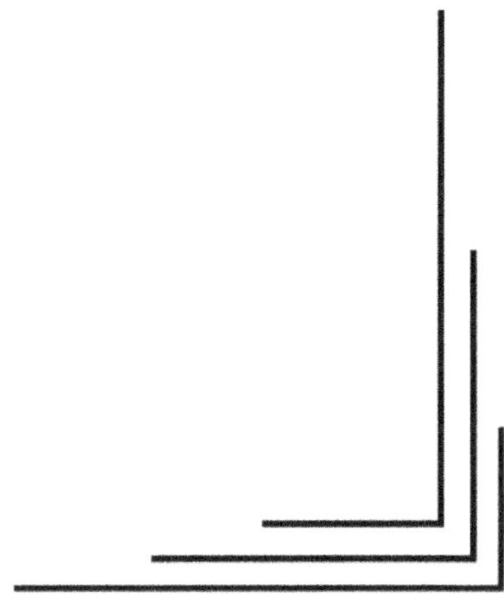

Suffering

Robert Kenion

"Sin will take you farther than you want to go, keep you longer than you want to stay, and cost you more than you want to pay."

This quote is attributed to Ravi Zacharias (1946-2020), the founder of Ravi Zacharias International Ministries and a world renowned Christian evangelical minister and apologist, whom it was discovered posthumously had engaged in habitual sexual misconduct. The number of people affected by the discovery of Minister Zacharias' sexual sins was multiple millions. This chapter addresses the issues and penalties of suffering related to two types of sin: secret sexual sin, and redeemed sin. Because humanity is born with a sin nature and a propensity or a desire to sin continuously, men must be particularly careful to confront these issues and confess them before God.

Suffering has multiple meanings. Sometimes the word suffer means to allow something to happen. In Matthew 19:14 Jesus said to the disciples:

> *Suffer little children, and forbid them not, to come unto me: for of such is the kingdom of heaven.*

In Psalm 121: 1-3 reads:

> *I will lift up mine eyes unto the hills, from whence cometh my help. My help cometh from the LORD, which made heaven and earth. He will not suffer thy foot to be moved: he that keepeth thee will not slumber.*

However, most of the time the word suffer means to undergo hardship, to endure persecution, to experience need, want, or painful sensations, alone or together with someone. What is interesting is that God uses both definitions of suffering to develop us, to discipline us, and to deliver us from evil and to become more like Jesus Christ. God "suffers" (allows) us to experience "suffering" (hardship and painful sensations) to preserve and permit our right to choose, even if we choose sin, and to demonstrate His love for us, to redeem mankind, given our choice to sin.

Taken from the Greek word "makrothumia," long-suffering means patient, endurance, not prone to quick or rash decisions or emotional impulsivity. God is long-suffering. We are encouraged in Hebrews 12: 1-2, to complete our race, to the glory of God:

> *Wherefore seeing we also are compassed about with so great a cloud of witnesses, let us lay aside every weight, and the sin which doth so easily beset us, and let us run with patience the race that is set before us. Looking unto Jesus the author and finisher of our faith; who for the joy that was set before him endured the cross, despising the shame, and is set down at the right hand of the throne of God.*

Secret Sexual Sin

Much of my suffering was self-inflicted and very painful. Early in my life I was heavily involved in secret sexual sins. My introduction to sexual sin was looking at naked women. Like the voyeur David, who, when he observed the wife of Uriah bathing, was overtaken with excitement and lust, I became a towering inferno of promiscuity. Let did I know; it would take almost twenty years to extinguish this inferno.

In my first marriage I was not physically unfaithful or adulterous. However, I was engaged in emotional infidelity. In today's vernacular I was a sexual addict. My life was consumed and revolved around fulfilling my sexual agendas, appetites, and addictions. Though I engrossed myself in daily rituals, routines, and practices associated with sexual addiction – watching pornographic movies, masturbation, and intensely focused on sexual fantasy, my gratification was generally short-lived. I existed in an empty, miserable, and self-loathing environment.

My sexual compulsions were always with me, despite the negative consequences I experienced. I lived in a world filled with guilt, shame, and disgust. My first wife was intolerant of my attitudes and behaviors and eventually divorced me. Over time I lost my wife, jobs, and at times became homeless, sleeping in the church. I tried to ignore the problem, pretend that I did not have a problem, or blame others for my problems. However, until I faced my problems head on and admitted that I was powerless over the "stronghold" of sexual sin, I would remain trapped and doomed.

A man cave is a very dangerous place for an undisciplined and un-discipled man. The purpose of a man cave is there's a designated part of the house designed for privacy, seclusion, and personal relaxation. In a man cave you might believe you have secluded yourself from God. Privacy does not apply to God nor are man caves off limits to Him. God does not wink at sin, consent to sin or "suffer" sin to go unpunished. God warns us of sin, and we should not take lightly or ignore His warnings.

Redeemed Sin

When sin remains secret, you remain sick. You cannot heal until your secrets are no longer secrets. The first person you must tell, full transparency, is God, Who is faithful to forgive us and cleanse us of all unrighteousness. In 2 Peter 3: 9 we are encouraged that the product of repentance is forgiveness:

> *The Lord is not slack concerning his promise, as some men count slackness; but is longsuffering to us-ward, not willing that any should perish, but that all should come to repentance.*

Suffering to obtain the will of God and for the cause of Christ leads to strength, growth, and spiritual maturity. Through the redemptive power of the Holy Spirit, I have reconciled with my former wife, my children, and other family and friends who were hurt by my behaviors. Most importantly, I now have a redeemed spirit and moral integrity. Truly, I can say, when I am weak His strength is perfect in me.

If you attempt to fight your battles in secret, with personal indiscretions or overt blatant sin, you will lose the battle every time. You will suffer continued pain, heartaches, and frustrations. You're reading this chapter because you have just made an appointment with God to have a "tell-it-all" session. What you will find is that if you suffer (experience pain) without God you will continue to suffer. But, if you suffer (allow) God to minister to you, then you will experience love, joy, and peace in ways you have never experienced. Blessings to you, my brothers!

Galatians 5: 16-25

> *This I say then, Walk in the Spirit, and ye shall not fulfil the lust of the flesh. For the flesh lusteth against the Spirit, and the Spirit against the flesh: and these are contrary the one to the other: so that ye cannot do the things that ye would. But if ye be led of the Spirit, ye are not under the law. Now the works of the flesh are manifest, which are these; Adultery, fornication, uncleanness, lasciviousness, Idolatry, witchcraft, hatred, variance, emulations,*

wrath, strife, seditions, heresies, Envyings, murders, drunkenness, revellings, and such like: of the which I tell you before, as I have also told you in time past, that they which do such things shall not inherit the kingdom of God.

But the fruit of the Spirit is love, joy, peace, longsuffering, gentleness, goodness, faith, Meekness, temperance: against such there is no law. And they that are Christ's have crucified the flesh with the affections and lusts. If we live in the Spirit, let us also walk in the Spirit.

Elder Robert Kenion is the father of three awesome children and the grandfather of four beautiful grandchildren. Born in Ardmore, PA, Elder Kenion graduated from the Haverford Township school system. After graduation, he enlisted in the United States Army where he faithfully served for six years. Elder Kenion was honorably discharged, achieving the rank of Sergeant.

Elder Kenion acknowledged and accepted his call into the ministry in 1991. He was ordained by and continues to serve his spiritual father, Overseer Jay T. Harrison, Sr.

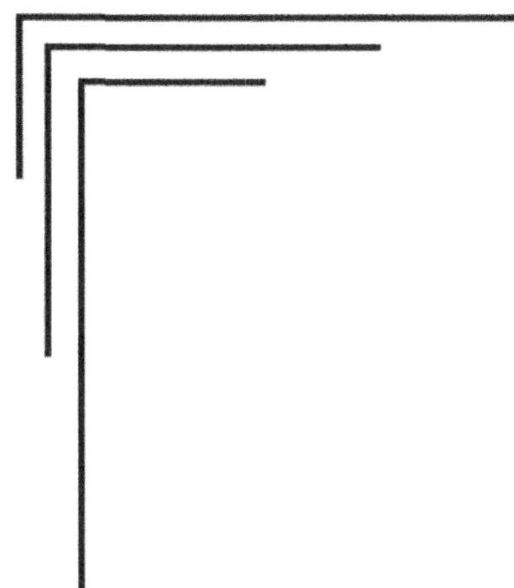

Chapter Eight

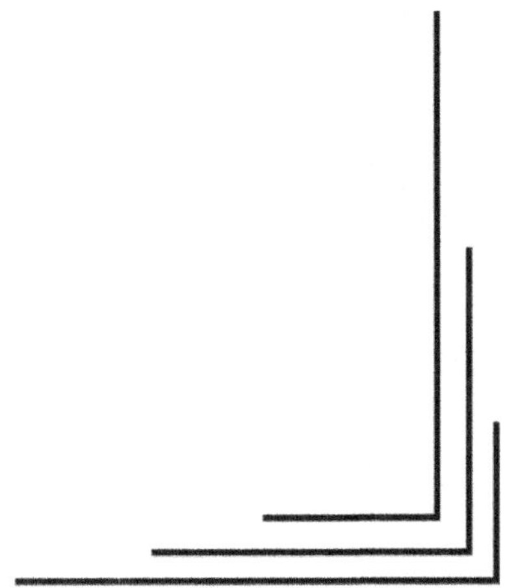

Forgiveness

Jay T. Harrison, Sr. and Micah Harrison

Deliver me, I pray thee, from the hand of my brother, from the hand of Esau: for I fear him, lest he come and smite me, and the mother with the children.

Genesis 32: 11

I can't stop thinking about the trait of forgiveness now after almost concluding this book on ten traits of a Man of God. I had nearly overlooked the one trait that made it possible for each author to write a contributing chapter to this book. More important than our literary contributions is that we can worship God and have the indwelling presence of the Holy Spirit with us.

Forgiveness is the expressed love of God given to us by Grace.
One of Jesus' final requests of His Father, while hanging nailed to the cross, in Luke 23: 34:

> *Then Jesus said, 'Father, forgive them; for they do not know what they're doing.*

What we hope that you will discover, learn, and understand is that true forgiveness is a spiritual exercise which requires the help of Holy Spirit for man to preform it. Forgiveness is what give us access to God. Jesus tells us in Matthew 6: 14-15:

> *Unless we forgive others, our Heavenly Father will not Forgive us.*

So, it's a requirement! We cannot afford not to exercise this act of love if we expect to have a guilt free and peaceful life.
Jesus, God's mercy wrapped in human flesh, often spoke about forgiveness. 1 John 4; 10-11 reads:

> *We love Him because He first loved us! In this is love, not that we loved God but that he loved us and sent his Son to be the atoning sacrifice for our sins. Beloved, since God loved us so much, we also ought to love one another.*

I'm sure you've heard the adage, "forgive and forget." If you're like most folk, you also heard the next phrase, "I can forgive you, but I may not forget!" Forgiveness is a difficult thing to do and harder still to commit to it. Scars, memories, old friends, and lingering enemies sometimes bring back constant reminders of the pain and abuse you received or the pain and abuse you delivered.

In the Hebrew language there are three words for forgiveness: **kaphar** (to cover or to purge), **naga'** (to lift, to carry or to take away), and **salach** (divine pardon). In Greek there are four words for forgiveness:

aphiemi (to cancel, to send away or to remit or pay), **aphesis** (to deliver from the penalty and the complete removal from the cause of the offense), **vicarious** (done on behalf of another or to take the place of another), and **propitiation** (the removal of God's anger and wrath).

True forgiveness is impossible for humans to do. We are born without the capacity to forgive. Our human nature is revenge, anger, control, and death and destruction. Biblically, wherever you read about an offense between to people you will find one person attempting to hurt or kill the other person. Only God has the capacity to truly forgive and only by the in-dwelling of the Holy Spirit can we truly forgive yourself and forgive others.

My twin sons, Mekhi and Micah, learned about the dangers and the destructive nature of personal offenses and what can happen when forgiveness is not part of their relationship. Unfortunately, these lessons cost the life of one of my sons.

On July 1, 2020, I received a distressing call from one of the sisters of True Vine Full Gospel Baptist Church. She informed me, in a panicked voice, that twins were riding around in a stolen car. She also told me that my wife was out driving in her car looking for them. Twenty minutes later I got another call from the same sister who initially called to tell me "Your boys were in a major car crash and it's all over Facebook!"

These words cut deep into my soul. I was numbed by the news. However, that was nothing compared to the rest of the story she shared. My heart seemed to stop when she continued, "They are doing CPR on one of the boys now!" One of my twin sons, Mekhi, was seriously injured in an automobile accident. Everything seemed to be moving fast, though I am not sure how much time had elapsed since I received the news. My wife rushed into the house saying, "It's not looking good." She didn't know if Mekhi was going to make it!"

While our boys were at the hospital, Mekhi, in a coma, was fighting for his life. His twin brother, Micah, was in a different room. Chester police officers and the hospital staff was trying to question him regarding the accident. Approximately four hours later my wife Crystal came home with Micah. Unassuming and carefree Micah walked into my room, smiled, and said, “I'm home!”

Bewildered, I asked him, “Where is Mekhi?” Micah responded, “He is still at the hospital.” Micah had not bothered to check on his brother before coming home. Crystal followed behind Micah and said with concern and irritation, "Your brother died, and they had to do CPR to bring him back! He's now on life support fighting for his life!" Those words paralyzed Micah. He walked away and went into their bedroom and lay on his brother's bed. He repeated that behavior, every day, for two months when his brother was in a coma. I believe for the first time Micah was threatened with the fragileness of life and that his brother was not indestructible or immortal.

I remember the day that Mekhi came out of the coma. Micah came into our bedroom and overheard the doctors talking to my wife on the phone about the road of recovery that lies ahead for Mekhi. Micah went walking back into their bedroom and laid down again. Only this time, he cried. I am not sure why he cried, was he thankful his prayers were answered, or guilt for the feelings he had for his twin brother, I’m not sure. It was the first time that Micah showed any outward emotion concerning his brother. About two weeks later his brother Mekhi came home from the hospital after undergoing rehabilitation. Mekhi was still in really bad shape. He broke every bone in his face and damaged his eyes. He had a trach in his throat. We were all happy to have Mekhi home, even Micah. Yet, the very next day Micah was back to picking and fighting with his brother Mekhi.

A few weeks after Mekhi returned home, I sat down in the boys’ room and listened to Micah tell his brother Mekhi what happened to him. Mekhi did not remember the accident and wondered why he was in the hospital when he came too. As Micah described the events of the day, Mekhi began to remember bits and pieces of the event but not the crash.

Mekhi even remembered saying, "I told them to stop the car and let me out! Micah responded in a very competitive street vernacular, "Yeah, you were crying like a baby!" I said, "No! He died and they had to restart his heart! Micah chimed in, with a cavalier attitude, "Oh well! that's on him. He should have never gotten in the car. If he had died that's on you bro, (referring to Mekhi)."

I wanted to knock all the teeth out Micah's mouth! I said, "Boy you are full of the devil! You're cold as ice! That's your brother! You hate yourself that much?" I told Mekhi to stop following his brother, "It's a dead end!' This road he is on will lead to death. As time went on Mekhi's recovery was progressing surprisingly fast. The doctors were surprised how well Mekhi was doing, commenting on how quickly his motor skills and his ability to talk returned! It was during his recovery that I realized the severity of Mekhi's injuries. Educationally, Mekhi had to complete his schoolwork virtually and was performing great! Because Mekhi was doing well in school and that led to a lot of arguments with his brother Micah, who was not doing so well at that time. Micah was especially bothered by all the attention going to his brother Mekhi.

Soon it was track and field season. Micah found something he could do that Mekhi couldn't do due to his health condition. Micah was an excellent athlete and would regularly taunt his brother who could not go outside because of covid concerns. As Micah excelled athletically, Mekhi excelled academically. Slowly and subtly, elements of the interpersonal competition that so defined their lives had returned.

Soon Mekhi was released from in-home care and allowed to return to school. That same weekend, Micah was on the track team, headed to the districts where he and his brother qualified for states. Yet, like in the past, Micah connected with the wrong crowd and got suspended from school. Micah was not permitted to attend the state track meet. Though Mekhi didn't place (come in first, second, or third place) in any event, he was able to physically recover and do what most physicians said he would not do again. "That's enough of a victory for me!" Mekhi said with the tone of a champion. Micah and Mekhi were now completely back at the daily competition of trying to determine who's the best.

Well, Mekhi decided to put an end to the competition. He asserted, "I'm not in competition with Micah, he's in competition with me. I'm the first, I'm smarter, I'm faster and even the better athlete, so he's trying to catch me I'm not trying do anything but be me!" It was that statement that fueled the rivalry between the two of them. Micah began hanging out with the wrong crowd and becoming involved in all sorts of illegal activities. Mekhi generally went looking for Micah to bring him home but ended up participating in some of the same things he saw his brother do.

I used to say that I could not imagine what those families are going through, raising juvenile delinquents. But having the privilege and honor to take on the responsibility of raising Micah and Mekhi now I do! Forgiveness was a must, for me and my wife, in our parenting relationship with our sons because from the very beginning we had to forgive them for behaviors and deeds that they learned as drug addicts and abandoned babies. I kept telling myself they don't know what they are doing. This is how they were born and shaped up until the age of four.

As they grew up living with us, we saw the impact that we had on them. However, once they entered the local public school system and had to attend school with the other students from the City of Chester, I recognized the direct conflict of morals and values that would confront our sons. The morality and values were completely different than what we were installing in them.

This placed the twins in a consistent need of parental forgiveness. It was the same forgiveness we need when we disregard and disobey the will of God. At times, it was difficult to provide a home and parental care for them. My wife and others began to fear what these boys might do. I wasn't afraid of them but I was afraid for them! Forgiveness kept me in the fight for their salvation.

We never gave up on them even though they would time and time again give up on us! Yet, we kept praying and waiting for the opportunity to love them despite their unwavering refusal to comply with any rules, at home, school, Court, probation, or detention. I would often warn them that the road they traveled will end in death if the system does not provide a facility to ensure you can live in a safe environment for juveniles.

I believe that our acceptance of God's love for us allowed my wife and me to share that same love with our sons. And when the unexpected tragic murder of our son Mekhi, by two of his childhood friends happened, Crystal and I turned to the Father again for the strength, courage, and peace to forgive the entire juvenile system that we spent years crying out for help with the twins.

The greatest challenge we had to face was the loss of our son Mekhi. The captain of detectives for the Chester police department called to let me know she needed to talk with me. My first thought was this call would be like all the other times before. We had received several calls from the police dealing with our sons due to their juvenile and criminal behavior. At the conclusion of each call, we would have to pick them up from the station or they would be dropped off at home. This time the police came and they came alone.

Mekhi, who had been living at the church for at least two weeks prior to his death, was making some positive changes in his life. He called me one day and asked if he could be in the program at the church called CHANGE. Mekhi said he was tired for being on the run and just hanging out. I told him, "If you're willing to change, which means follow the rules, then yes! I would love to have you be a part of the program!"

That was forgiveness, letting go and clearing the slate. Mekhi was doing so well and getting things in order. He was set to go to the Job Corps, but the streets refused to let him go. There was a young female assigned to keep track of him, and "line him up!" a street term for setting him up to be killed. One morning she texted Mekhi, to lure him out of the church alone.

The night his brother Micah was shot in the leg almost a year earlier Mekhi was there, standing right next to the shooter. He checked on his brother to make sure he was OK and then ran because he had a warrant and feared being arrested. Micah was home again now recovering and was up moving around in about five months. During that time we had not heard or seen Mekhi.

Once Micah was able to go outside and return to the neighborhood park to play basketball Mekhi and Micah reconnected. It took only a few days before both twins were out of the house running the streets. It was during that time that they began robbing and breaking into cars, homes, local businesses and using and dealing drugs. They were out of control! I even received a disturbing call from one of the local drug dealers letting me know, "that someone is going to kill your son, Micah! " He told us, "We needed to move, your family is not safe!" Both boys were in danger because they were identical twins and it was hard to tell them apart. Not many days after that call, Mekhi surfaced and told me it would be best if we moved. I told him, "that I will never run from the devil!" He apologized for all the trouble and negative energy he and his brother had brought to our family. He was looking for his brother to instruct him to lay low.

Micah, who was now at home on house arrest and his brother were going house to house looking for shelter. After several months had passed, both Mekhi and Micah were out again, this time it led to both being arrested and detained in juvenile detention programs. Mekhi had been in placement for six months before being released and sent to a mental health and Juvenile behavioral treatment center.

Mekhi, after ten days, was released and went right back out on the streets. He wrote a letter to us stating he was protecting us by staying away from home. Mekhi begged us to move because someone had threatened to come and kill him. Mekhi was on the run after that call for another two months before we saw him again. Micah was still in a juvenile state detention facility and had not seen his brother for at least six months. The two had only spoken briefly two or three times over the phone, apologizing to one another and instructing each other to get it together. They had made plans to return to school, to run track, and then go off to college.

Mekhi was still not staying at the house because he feared what potential harm his being at home might bring to the family. Eventually Mekhi had started living at the church and was doing well. Then one day he got a message on Instagram where one of his neighborhood friends threatened to hurt everyone there at the Church if he didn't come and see what he wanted. After receiving a text message from this young girl, who had been hanging around, Mekhi left the church at approximately 4:30 AM before our breakfast and group meeting.

The police informed me that Mekhi was killed by a single gunshot to the chest. My son was dead! He was not coming home; not going to the Job Corps. He was gone! I began to worship and sing "Jireh you are enough, I will be content in every circumstance, you are more than enough!" The police asked if they could pray for me and my family. The power of God filled my office. I knew the protection and presence of God was with me. The detective informed me that they knew it was one of Mekhi's friends. I said Father forgive them for they don't know what they are doing! You must arrest them but I'm praying that My Father forgives and that they are saved!

The weight of this loss I laid at the Father's feet. His love strengthened and comforted us to walk through this valley of the shadow of death. I can't really explain how we were able to come to a posture of forgiveness so quickly. Even before we really had the chance to mourn

Mekhi's death All I can say is that the power of His love made forgiveness possible. Even during the funeral service standing face to face with some of the very youth who indirectly were involved in our son's death, our hearts were filled with compassion and forgiveness towards them and a desire that they might be saved.

One of the greatest traits of God has given to mankind is the gift of forgiveness. The fact that God has not given us justice, that is, He has given us what we *really deserve*, is one of the greatest expressions of His love for us. He instead loved us with a grace that is so amazing. Ephesians 4:32 reads:

> "And be ye kind one to another, tenderhearted, forgiving one another, even as God for Christ's sake hath forgiven you."

When I think about this trait of forgiveness the best biblical story that most accurately describes Mekhi and Micah is Jacob and his twin brother Esau who were rivals from the time they were in their mother's womb and continued their rivalry after they were born. I am so happy that our twin son Micah was willing to submit the letter he wrote to his twin brother, Mekhi James Harrison, who was senselessly murdered on January 25, 2023, by a childhood friend and his female accomplice. Micah's letter literally moved me to tears because it was so powerful to listen to the love, forgiveness, and innocence that he experienced from his brother throughout their relationship and prayerfully he will demonstrate towards others and especially towards himself.

In this letter you will witness the power of forgiveness. Two identical twin brothers who spent most of the time in competition with each other over literally everything! Who was first, and who was the best? The writer, my son Micah expresses how the transition of his brother though painful is an opportunity to pursue purpose. The letter also provides a lesson in learning how to forgive, to divinely pardon, to deliver from the penalty of the offense, to let things go, to cancel a debt, to and enjoy the liberty of freedom in life that can be found, only in Jesus Christ!

Letter written to Mekhi Harrison from his twin brother Micah Harrison who was killed on January 25, 2023.

Mekhi James Harrison, a Legend. Before a lot of you knew him, I did and that's the best part about this. I know him best! Mekhi was strong, smart, the bravest person I know, and eager. If his mind was set, no matter the environment, what he imagined was what he accomplished. Mekhi was the most passionate and caring person ever, and my favorite attribute about him was even when it seemed like he didn't care, he really did. So, whenever we argued or fought, he would ignore me, and I always knew if I keep pestering him the love and care he had for me would eventually show. My brother was my everything, Batman, and Robin, he was Batman. It was always me second questioning things.

Envy is the only reason this is the last time I'll see my brother. It's rare, very rare to come past people who didn't like him. His bold, funny character always stood up and out. Mekhi was a hero, he was a legend, one of a kind. Envy and hate aren't something you do to ordinary everyday people; you hate someone who is better than you. Envied by many. I hear the saying, "with great power comes great responsibility" but it also comes with jealous, weird, evil people. Mekhi had something to offer, and he gave us what he had to offer. Life, love, anger, stress, but what he gave me that stuck out, was to never take the people you care about for granted. Human traits are what he gave us.

Mekhi was the perfect person, including his imperfections, the imperfections is what made him even more perfect. It's a lot of things my brother did to make us angry, but only now have we learned to let certain things that made us upset go. Now we look back and wonder why we complained about the little stuff. Mekhi taught, at least to me, to let go and live life. You can't live life upset or grumpy, and no matter what he was going through, Mekhi always smiled. I lost my best friend, secret teller, heart, and my hero. But I gained braveness, honesty, trust, resilience, boldness, eagerness to achieve, and the peace of mind knowing my brother will always be okay now and no one can hurt him. Today is the first time I'm seeing my brother in 8 months, now I know he will never leave me and keep protecting me like he always has. I didn't lose anyone today; I only lost my selfishness and doubt in everyone. I know my life carries a better future, thanks to the person who ensured it. Mekhi wouldn't want us crying or mourning, he would want us dancing and celebrating like it was our last celebration.

It hurts knowing we will never play basketball or football together, but what doesn't hurt is knowing I can talk to Mekhi whenever I want. I can laugh at the things we did instead of worrying. Mekhi opened a lot of doors for all of us to do great things, and if you want to honor Mekhi you will walk through those doors. The heartache may end for some of you, some of you will forget my brother, some will constantly struggle with his new position in life, but I won't.

The heartache will never stop, I will never forget Mekhi and I will always thank him for the new chapter he opened for me. My life was probably going to go left, I felt like I had nothing to offer to anyone. I didn't have any motivation, and when I was at my lowest, like always, my brother came to the rescue. Now I am motivated and a reason to strive for better. The next couple of months I know will suck, it is going to be hard, but it will get better. I'll adapt to my new life.

Right now, it's hard for me, without judging, this is harder on me than anyone. The words I'm saying are from the heart, my brain just must get in sync. To the legend, this very specific, handcrafted legend, I will always dread in our memories, we had one of the best roller coaster rides. Those rides defined our relationship, every tear, punch, swear, sweat, smile; every time we felt fear, agony, tired, left out like outsiders, it created men and the worst part is the best man always goes too soon. I heard this but now I know it's true, "All legends fall in the making," Mekhi was the one who let me in on that quote. He knew the risk, but only legends make the sacrifice.

I love you and it's a lot of people who do. You are the greatest thing that ever happened to me. You became the way when there wasn't, and I will always be grateful. I heard someone say never mistake salt for sugar, you turned my salt into sugar. We all will reminisce in your memories, but we all are thankful for you giving us these precious memories, but even more thankful for the new chapter you gave us. Mekhi James Harrison, now known as "Khi the Legend". I love you with everything. Continue to guide me forever bruh!

Oh, what joy for those whose disobedience is forgiven, whose sin is put out of sight! Yes, what joy for those whose record the LORD has cleared of guilt, whose lives are lived in complete honesty!

Psalm 32: 1-2 (New Living Translation)

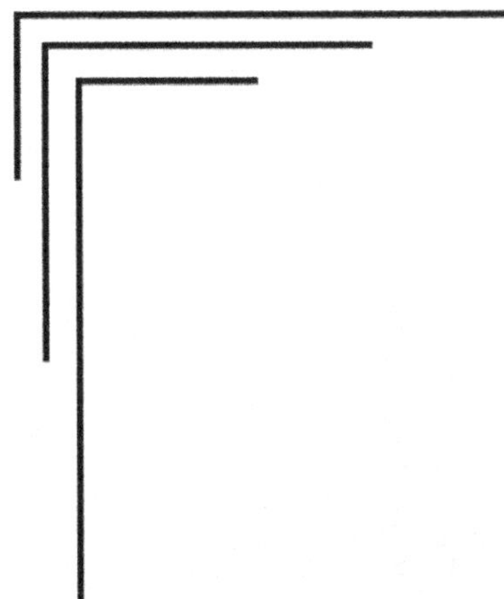

Chapter Nine

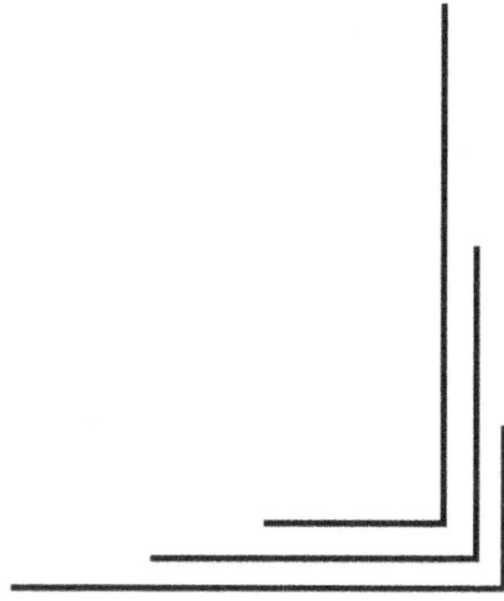

Provider

Robert Jamison, Sr.

All over the world Christians of every background have been captivated by the name Jireh of Jehovah-Jireh. Contemporary Christian Music (CCM) has integrated the name into their music, such that you can sing songs articulating the theme *The Lord will provide.* This characteristic of God, found in Genesis 22, is essential to our understanding of God and His love for us. The characteristic of the provider can vividly be seen in the behavior of God our Father and in our Lord Jesus Christ. To better understand the role of provider a quick review of the text in Genesis 22: 5-14 is in order:

> *And Abraham said unto his young men, Abide ye here with the ass; and I and the lad will go yonder and worship, and come again to you.*

And Abraham took the wood of the burnt offering and laid it upon Isaac his son; and he took the fire in his hand, and a knife; and they went both of them together. And Isaac spake unto Abraham his father, and said, My father: and he said, Here am I, my son. And he said, Behold the fire and the wood: but where is the lamb for a burnt offering?

And Abraham said, My son, God will provide himself a lamb for a burnt offering: so they went both of them together.

And they came to the place which God had told him of; and Abraham built an altar there, and laid the wood in order, and bound Isaac his son, and laid him on the altar upon the wood. And Abraham stretched forth his hand and took the knife to slay his son.

And the angel of the LORD called unto him out of heaven, and said, Abraham, Abraham: and he said, Here am I. And he said, Lay not thine hand upon the lad, neither do thou anything unto him: for now I know that thou fearest God, seeing thou hast not withheld thy son, thine only son from me.

And Abraham lifted his eyes, and looked, and behold behind him a ram caught in a thicket by his horns: and Abraham went and took the ram and offered him up for a burnt offering in the stead of his son.

And Abraham called the name of that place Jehovah Jireh: as it is said to this day, In the mount of the LORD it shall be seen.

The Hebrew word for provide is raah, pronounced *raw-aw*, has some very unusual definitions. The term raah or provide used in Genesis 22:8 means advise self, approve, to take heed, to present, to regard, to have respect, and cause to see or perceive. The ram caught in the thicket was a foreshadowing of the sacrificial atonement and substitutionary offering of Jesus Christ as the Lamb of God. In Genesis 22 God asked Abraham to sacrifice his son and Abraham obeyed. However, the presentation of Isaac was an insufficient and unnecessary sacrifice because the death of

Isaac was not redemptive and could not take away the sins of the world. It would be approximately 4000 years later when John the Baptist, recorded in John 1: 29 declares:

> *The next day John seeth Jesus coming unto him, and saith, Behold the Lamb of God, which taketh away the sin of the world.*

As we see in the accounts of Abraham and Isaac, your faith, like Abraham and Isaac's faith, will be tested. One of the greatest challenges is not knowing or understanding where God is taking you, but trusting and believing the Lord will provide.

Learning the character of God as a provider started when I was called into ministry. My first assignment was a Psalm 23 experience. I was called to lead people into green pastures, that is, to help them improve their lives and the conditions of their community. My second assignment was to invest in people and to treat them fairly. The burden of this calling was overwhelming, but being in ministry for almost 40 years, I have learned to trust God.

We are blessed to be a blessing. Believers are part of the Abrahamic covenant established in Genesis and is now manifested in my life. Being a blessing means I am a giver. The God characteristic of provision is a trait I embodied. Every day I put my foot on floor is a testimony to God as my provider. Fifteen years ago I received a terminal diagnosis of cancer. I was told that I only had 6 months to live, but here I am today, sharing God's goodness with you. God provided Jesus and Jesus provided the stripes by which I was healed (Isaiah 53: 5 and 1 Peter 2: 24).

Provision is Revealed in the Path of Obedience

Knowing God as provider requires that you remain patient. It takes patience to endure life's experiences and challenges. Dictionary.com defines patience as the capacity to accept or tolerate delay, trouble, or suffering without getting angry or upset.

Think about it.... how many times have you needed or wanted something from God, and it felt as though God was taking His sweet old time to respond to your urgent need or request?! As a giver, you must be willing to wait for God. Provision is revealed in the path of obedience. The provision of the ram in the bush was discovered due to the faith and obedience of Abraham and Isaac. Remember this very important point. Abraham knew the purpose of their trip to mount Moriah. Isaac learned of the purpose on Mount Moriah. Listen to the faith of Abraham:

> *And Abraham said unto his young men, Abide ye here with the ass; and I and the lad will go yonder and worship, and come again to you.*

Abraham had faith he articulated, and Isaac demonstrated the works of faith when he willingly submitted to his father Abraham. God intervened when Abraham raised his hand to sacrifice Isaac. Points to remember from this passage:

1. Abraham and Isaac had faith.
2. Abraham and Isaac obeyed.
3. Abraham and Isaac's faith were tested.
4. God provided Himself

I have the responsibility to share with others how to succeed in giving. A big part of this discussion will be encouraging and developing self-control. Just because God has made you promise, the promise does not exempt you from pain, suffering, and hardship. As a matter of fact, because God has made you promise, you should expect to be challenged. It is important during your challenging season, to keep your eyes faith-focused on God. Do not lose your focus. Remember God has provided and will provide. I encourage you with words found in Psalm 27: 13-14:

> *I had fainted unless I had believed to see the goodness of the* Lord *in the land of the living. Wait on the* Lord*: be of good*

> *courage, and he shall strengthen thine heart: wait, I say, on the LORD.*

Providers Have the Ability to Access the Needs of Others

In January 2018, I was afforded the opportunity to visit and spend two weeks in Liberia. Early one morning I was sitting on the balcony overlooking the community where I was staying. As I observed the community, watching the children make their way to school, the Lord reminded me that these are His people.

I noticed how they were walking in the rain without umbrellas, raincoats, or rain boots. The necessities that most Americans take for granted; they did not have, nor did they have access to get what they needed. I wanted to help. I asked the Lord what to do. The Holy Spirit led me to ask my congregation and fellow pastors to assist in the endeavor to provide umbrellas, raincoats, and rainboots to the Liberian people in the community where I was staying. We were able to provide enough supplies to get them through the rainy season. Points to remember:

1. Access the need
2. Ask God for a plan
3. Execute the plan

Providers Travel in Unchartered Territory

When Abraham and Isaac began their journey, they were traveling in uncharted territory. Genesis 22: 1-4:

> *And it came to pass after these things, that God did tempt Abraham, and said unto him, Abraham: and he said, Behold, here I am.*
>
> *And he said, Take now thy son, thine only son Isaac, whom thou lovest, and get thee into the land of Moriah; and offer him there*

> *for a burnt offering upon one of the mountains which I will tell thee of.*
>
> *And Abraham rose early in the morning, and saddled his ass, and took two of his young men with him, and Isaac his son, and clave the wood for the burnt offering, and rose up, and went unto the place of which God had told him. Then on the third day Abraham lifted up his eyes and saw the place afar off.*

The true test of givers is obedience. Sometimes your obedience will lead you to and through unchartered territories. God wants to take you to places that are unfamiliar to you to bless you and for you to bless others.

When it comes to giving financially, most believers find this difficult to execute. Jesus said in Matthew 6: 19-21:

> *Lay not up for yourselves treasures upon earth, where moth and rust doth corrupt, and where thieves break through and steal: But lay up for yourselves treasures in heaven, where neither moth nor rust doth corrupt, and where thieves do not break through nor steal: For where your treasure is, there will your heart be also.*

We must learn to give even when it is uncomfortable to do so. It is hard to give when you do not understand how you will survive. I challenge you, when God instructs you to give and the math doesn't add up, give anyway. What I have learned when I give when it does not make sense, God provides a blessing that does not make sense either. He continually provides exceedingly, abundantly more than I can ask, or think according to the power that works in me.

Luke 6:38, Jesus said:

> *Give and it shall be given unto you: good measure, pressed down, shaken together, and running over, shall men give unto your bosom. For with the same measure that ye mete withal it shall be measured to you again.*

Providers Must Have Unshakable Faith

I do not know if I can express enough how faith is the driving force behind my heart of giving. My spirit of wanting to help others is because I believe what God says about you and me! The Scriptures are full of examples of what unshakable faith looks like. Let's take a moment to look at a few:

- In Genesis 22 the faith of Abraham is tested when God asked him to sacrifice his so Isaac.
- In Exodus 14 the faith of Moses is tested as the nation of Israel is led through the Red Sea.
- In Daniel 6 the faith of Daniel is tested as he
- in a lion's den. Daniel's commitment and faith in God landed him in a place that should have killed him, but God provided.
- In Esther 4 the faith of Esther is tested as she approached the king on behalf of her people.

Providers Demonstrate the Love of God Through Compassionate Giving

Providers are lovers! Love is an action; an insatiable desire to give. Love is foundational to our understanding of who is a provider and what a provider does. A provider offers love, and the love is unusually manifested in things. Remember, it is not the created things we honor but the Creator. Romans 5:8 "But God commendeth his love towards us, in that, while we were yet sinners, Christ died for us."

As God demonstrated His love towards us, we must demonstrate our love towards others. As God's love does not show partiality, neither should our love be partial nor limited. You must be intentional about showing love. We should be concerned with the sufferings and misfortunes of others. We should be empathetic. We must put ourselves and their shoes and do unto them as we would want someone to do unto us. Sounds familiar, right?

We cannot sit in our usual church box and just pray for people. Praying is good, but God calls us to action. We are to live out the gospel. Remember in Matthew 25, Jesus was sharing stories to help His followers understand what heaven would be like. You should read the entire chapter, but especially 34-40, Jesus said:

> *Then shall the King say unto them on his right hand, Come, ye blessed of my Father, inherit the kingdom prepared for you from the foundation of the world:*
>
> *For I was an hungred, and ye gave me meat: I was thirsty, and ye gave me drink: I was a stranger, and ye took me in: Naked, and ye clothed me: I was sick, and ye visited me: I was in prison, and ye came unto me.*
>
> *Then shall the righteous answer him, saying, Lord, when saw we thee an hungred, and fed thee? or thirsty, and gave thee drink?*
>
> *When saw we thee a stranger, and took thee in? or naked, and clothed thee? Or when saw we thee sick, or in prison, and came unto thee?*
>
> *And the King shall answer and say unto them, Verily I say unto you, Inasmuch as ye have done it unto one of the least of these my brethren, ye have done it unto me.*

Providers are Visionary

Habakkuk 2:2 And the LORD answered me: "Write the vision; make it plain on the tablets, so he may run that readeth it." The world now creates vision boards. Vision boards put a visual to the strategic plans they have created to accomplish their life goals. You must do the same with what God has shown you. You want to make sure you and your community or congregational partners have a plan to become givers or to become better givers. "Without a vision, the people perish." (Proverbs 29). As a leader and one who wants to develop givers, you should be able to show them step-by-step on how to become a giver or increase their giving.

Conclusion

To be a provider/giver, you must emulate Christ's actions. You must see people as He sees people, and act according to His word. It would benefit us all to be reminded of the saying that came out a few years ago, "What Would Jesus Do?" When you don't know what to do, simply ask: What would Jesus do? and act accordingly. In His Service.

Robert Jamison, 75 years young, is the Senior Pastor, Fairview Full Gospel Baptist Church. Fairview Full Gospel Baptist Church was founded in 1997, birthed from the passion and dedication of Pastor Jamison to fulfill his God-given purpose and assignment.

Pastor Jamison was born in South Carolina in July 1947.

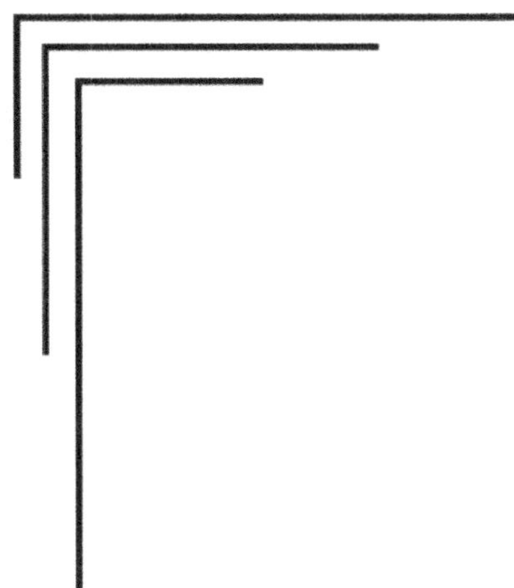

Chapter Ten

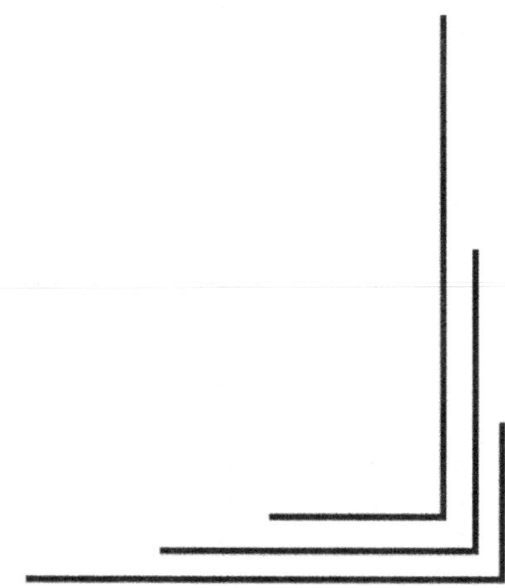

Worship

Vincent Smith

Early one Sunday morning a mother encouraged her six-year-old daughter, "Hurry yourself so we won't be late for worship service." While hurrying to get dressed the young girl asked her mother inquisitively, "What is worship?" The mother responded with a religious traditional perspective of worship. She said, "Worship is what we do in church when we sing, dance, and clap our hands to let God know that He is special to us and that we love Him!" The mother knew immediately that her answer was inadequate. She pondered, wondering if she had reduced worship to s set of physical activities that only happened in church on Sundays. What is worship, why should we worship, and why is God looking for worshippers in His kingdom.

The bible is filled with scriptures concerning the subject of worship. In the Old Testament the Hebrew word for worship is *SHACHAH* (shaw-khaw), which means to bow down, fall or lay prostrate in homage to one who is superior (GOD). In the New Testament the Greek word for worship is *PROSKUNEO* (pros-koo-neh), meaning to fawn or crouch, or to prostrate oneself.

Worship is the result of coming to know the true and living GOD. It is an intimate relationship and an ongoing fellowship with God where He reveals Himself to us. Our worship with and for God is demonstrated in many ways such as communal service, personal sacrifice, and reverential adoration found in praise, song, dance, and testimony. In Romans 12: 1-2, Apostle Paul uses an incredible verb to emphasize the importance of worship:

> *I **beseech** you therefore, brethren, by the mercies of God, that ye present your bodies a living sacrifice, holy, acceptable unto God, which is your reasonable service. And be not conformed to this world: but be ye transformed by the renewing of your mind, that ye may prove what is that good, and acceptable, and perfect, will of God.*

Paul uses the beseech, which means beg. The will of God is that we worship Him and according to God, this is our *"reasonable service."* What is amazing is that God provides mercies or opportunities for the believer to present our lives as a living sacrifice. The presentation of our bodies can be a struggle.

As men, we want to do our "thang!" We create kingdoms or man caves where we are the sovereign rulers. We design these kingdoms to serve our needs and desires, to provide comfort and security, and if we are not careful, we will worship the created things, the 72-inch flat screen television, the Lexus RX 350 F series, and the personally tailored PINI Parma suits, above the Creator.

How can I worship a holy GOD, a God I have never seen, and that I don't really know? I worship God because I know I was unable to find God, to satisfy the debt of sin credited to my account and keep me from returning to an unholy sinful life and nature. God's eternal plan was designed to win and woo us back to Himself. A Holy God in pursuit of sinful man. Therefore, Paul begs us to change our thinking about our relationship with God.

In our fallen state, due to sin, we all seek to make our own gods. These gods are created to suit our own likings, gods who we can control, who won't tell us "no" or tell us what we can and cannot do, gods who make no real demands or commands that make us uncomfortable. Yet, while we were making gods for ourselves God developed a plan, found in Isaiah 53 and the method to execute that plan:

> *All we like sheep have gone astray; we have turned everyone to his own way; and the LORD hath laid on him the iniquity of us all. He was oppressed, and he was afflicted, yet he opened not his mouth: he is brought as a lamb to the slaughter, and as a sheep before her shearers is dumb, so he openeth not his mouth.*
>
> *He was taken from prison and from judgment: and who shall declare his generation? for he was cut off out of the land of the living: for the transgression of my people was he stricken. And he made his grave with the wicked, and with the rich in his death; because he had done no violence, neither was any deceit in his mouth.*
>
> *Yet it pleased the LORD to bruise him; he hath put him to grief: when thou shalt make his soul an offering for sin, he shall see his seed, he shall prolong his days, and the pleasure of the LORD shall prosper in his hand. He shall see of the travail of his soul and shall be satisfied: by his knowledge shall my righteous servant justify many; for he shall bear their iniquities.*

So, I read in this love letter written by Isaiah, the heart of a loving father. In this letter I not only found out about my father – Abba, but I find Him. I find the living and loving God through His living word. I discovered that God desires to have a relationship and continuous fellowship with me so much so that HE sent His Son Jesus, who became the living sacrifice, holy and acceptable to God. I now realize that I am being pursued by Him and prepared for that which HE called me to – worship. I am a recipient of His love, grace, and mercy.

I must confess it wasn't always that way for me. I had to grow in my walk with the LORD. In my early years I was on fire for Jesus! Like any new relationship, the fire burned bright just on enthusiasm alone. I was young and didn't understand that like every relationship some maintenance work is required. I wasn't prepared for, nor did I have the wisdom to ask for help when the issues of life became hard and then harder.

Being married with children, struggling to pay bills, not making enough money ***AND*** trying to make a home where Jesus was LORD, I confess to you right now was difficult! "I had no joy in my heart." To be brutally honest I wanted to know why JESUS wasn't doing something to fix the problems. I had real issues and it just seemed like worship for me was for the most part just a sense of duty.

Yes, there were times when praise and worship was a joyous experience. I can recall many good times during those early days. But as I look back and examine my walk with the LORD l must say that much of my joy in the LORD was due to outside influences such as maybe the choir sang my favorite song, some unexpected financial windfall. Outside circumstances seemed to dictate the depth of my worship experience.

My relationship with the LORD was superficial, casual, and conditional at best. I gradually walked away. I felt so far from GOD during those times. It was a dark time. You see, before I knew Jesus Christ, I was in darkness but didn't know it. I had fallen back into the hole that Jesus had pulled me out. I revisited some of the old habits, places, and people who were at one time the source of my existence. Paul encouraged new saints in the Church at Galatia (Galatians 5: 1):

> *Stand fast therefore in the liberty wherewith Christ hath made us free and be not entangled again with the yoke of bondage.*

I had become entangled again with the shackle and yoke of sin. I can honestly tell you that sin will:

1. take you farther than you are willing to go
2. cost you more than you are willing to spend and
3. keep you longer than you are willing to stay.

Before long I felt so lost and so alone that I could only cry out from the depth of my soul. I was desperate, hurting, and worst of all I was stuck. As I prayed for answers to questions that we all ask God – "Why am I in this mess?" – "God, if you love me, why did you let this happen to me?" and "How long will I have to suffer in this situation?"

Jesus answered me with a question: *"Why are you here?"* He kept this question before me so much so that I began to pray about this question. The first answer I got from Him concerning this question, is that He knows and cares where I am. I should not have to tell you how much that answer blessed me. It occurred to me that Jesus never left me, even in my rebellion going and coming in and out of places that I did not belong. *HE REALLY LOVES ME*, was my thought concerning this revelation.

Second, I was keenly aware that God had been waiting for me to cry out to Him. Not just a casual cry (God is not interested in a causal relationship with His children) but a cry from the depth of my soul – like the cry of a thirsty man lost in the desert crying for water or the cry of an acute asthmatic searching for air.

As He wooed me back into His loving arms, I discovered something very important: Worship is about a Savior who would call to Himself those who need healing, deliverance, fellowship, and rest. Worship is for God because He is worthy. Worship is also for us because in worship we can see the love of the Father more clearly.

"What's worship mean?" is the question my daughter asked her mother many years ago. I have given you the Hebrew and Greek definition, but I have learned it's more than knowing the terminologies. It's knowing the true and living God who has called us to worship Him. We know Him as He has revealed Himself through His Word. I pray that you will come to know the God of the bible. And in knowing Him you would reverence Him in your sacrifice of worship.

Consider the psalmist in the entire Psalm 119. The psalmist expresses tremendous honor and reverence about the Word of God and therefore the God of the word because the Word of God and the God of the word are the same (John 1: 1-3). The psalmist goes on and on proclaiming the connection between adoration, honor, reverence, and worship of the God the bible. As you read the many verses in the book of Psalm 119 it will become quite clear to you that the psalmist has fallen in love with the word of God and has fallen in love with God. The psalmist realizes, to his surprise, as he pursues the God who wrote this letter of love, that it is he who is being pursued by God (Psalm 119: 46-50):

> *I will speak of thy testimonies also before kings and will not be ashamed. And I will delight myself in thy commandments, which I have loved. My hands also will I lift up unto thy commandments, which I have loved; and I will meditate in thy statutes. Remember the word unto thy servant, upon which thou hast caused me to hope. This is my comfort in my affliction: for thy word hath quickened me.*

Reverend Vincent J. Smith, Sr. married his 8th grade sweetheart and 47 years later is still smitten by her love. Rev. Smith is the father of three children, grandfather of six children, and great grandfather of three children. He worked as an electrical contractor for 26 years.

Under the leadership of the late Reverend Charles Walker, Rev. Smith was licensed to preach in 1992 at the 19th Street Missionary Baptist Church, Philadelphia, PA. Burdened with a ministry to serve youth and introduce them to Jesus Christ, Rev. Smith passionately pursues his calling.

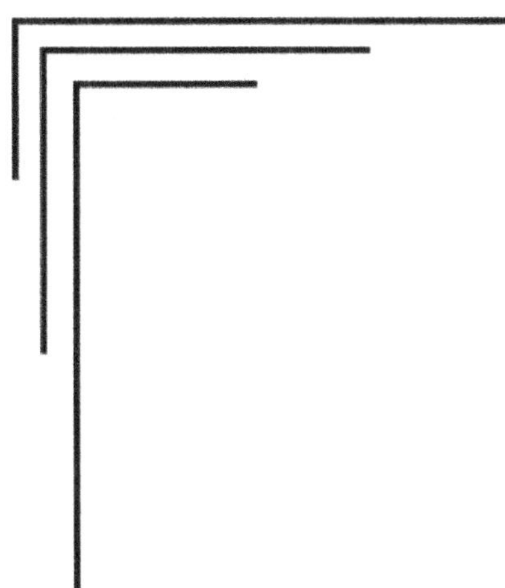

Epilogue

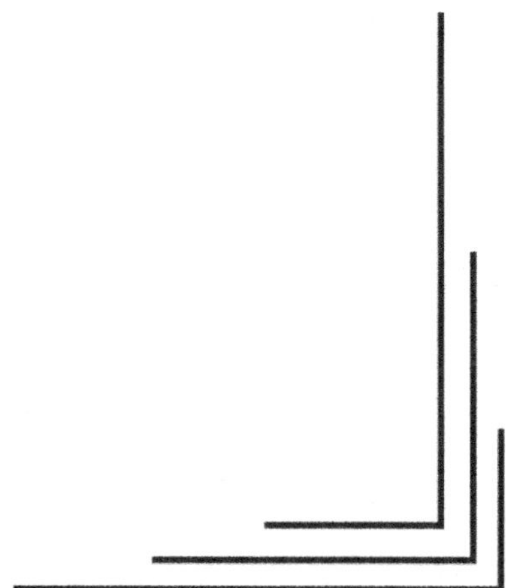

Jay T. Harrison, Sr.

Wow! What an amazing ride. Hopefully, you read the entire book. In each of the chapters the authors not only enlighten us on the various composite traits that help describe God and these same traits God has also entrusted to mankind. The Apostle Paul refers to mankind as God's greatest masterpiece. Notice what he says in Ephesians 2:10 (NLT):

> *For we are God 's masterpiece. He has created us anew in Christ Jesus, so we can do the good things he planned f or us long ago.*

God is so amazing that He even placed a treasure on the inside of us.

> *We now have this light shining in our hearts, but we ourselves are like fragile clay jars containing this great*
>
> *treasure. This makes it clear that our great power is from God, not from ourselves" (2 Corinthians 4:7 NLT).*

All the authors, whom I know personally, have overcome and prevailed the trials and testing of their faith that manifested the characteristics of God. I hope and pray that what was revealed will assist in helping you overcome the challenges you may be facing now or will at some point in your future. Let 's recap some of the key points from each chapter that will assist us in understanding the rich deposit of Godliness that our Heavenly Father has bestowed upon us. So, let's review!

Chapter One: The Image of God

1. We are created in the image of God, possessive of dominion, power, and authority to speak intelligently like God, through the anointing of the Holy Spirit.
2. The image of God is the expression of God's love for human creation towards us; through the shed blood of Jesus Christ who has redeemed and restored us to Sonship whereby we cry Abba Father.
3. Therefore, we are sons of God, empowered by the Holy Spirit to walk in our purpose, fulfill our assignment and accomplish greater works while we are alive.

Chapter Two: The Likeness of God

1. We are created in the likeness of God to function or operate just like Him with the ability to think, decree, rule and subdue the earth.
2. The likeness of God means to compare, resemble, model or to be similar to God, but mankind is not God; although we are His workmanship, created in Christ Jesus for good works, which God prepared beforehand, that we should walk in them according to *(Ephesians 2:10 NKJV).*
3. As a man of God, it's important for you to know and believe that God has a unique plan and purpose for your life no matter what has happened in your past or what is currently happening in the moment. Just like Jacob who strived with God, with men and

eventually prevailed; God is changing your name to fit your new identity.

Chapter Three: The Dominion and Authority of God

1. Dominion is power or the use of power through the authority of the word of God contained in our position and identity as men of God. Jesus made it very clear when He said, all authority in heaven and on earth has been given to me according to (Matthew 28:18 NIV).
2. To operate in the fullness of dominion and authority requires a changing of the mind towards kingdom thinking; where we must free, feed and focus our minds.
3. God has given mankind dominion and authority to govern and manage His affairs on the earth. We must occupy until He comes.

Chapter Four: The Blessing of God

1. The blessing of God is immediately bestowed upon us when we receive the unending, everlasting love of the Father.
2. The blessing is an empowerment, an endorsement, and an enrichment of the power of God to help us fulfill the plan of God.
3. Because of the blessing our sin is not larger than His grace; there is no shame or condemnation and the gifts and calling of God are irrevocable which simply means God will not change His mind concerning you.

Chapter Five: The Faith of God

1. The most important power we possess on earth is our faith; therefore, faith comes by hearing and hearing by the word of God.
2. Faith never waits for perfect results; it always responds to the now. For now, faith is the substance of things hoped for, the evidence of things not seen according to Hebrews 11:1.

3. Refuse to pull the plug on your faith and believe God for the impossible. Jesus said if you can believe, all things are possible to him who believes according to Mark 9:23.

Chapter Six: Prayer

1. Prayer in its simplest form is communication with God. It's when you as a man of God express and share your thoughts, hurts and concerns with your heavenly Father. But in everything by prayer and supplication, with thanksgiving, let your requests be made known to God according to Philippians 4:6 (NKJV).
2. The trait of a God-fearing praying man is the evidence or fruit of his walk and connection to God.
3. A praying man prays according to the will and instruction of Jesus knowing that the effective, fervent prayer of a righteous man avails much according to James 5:16 (NKJV).

Chapter Seven: Suffering

1. To suffer means to allow something to happen, to undergo hardship, to experience need, want or to endure persecution.
2. Sometimes our suffering can be self-inflicted and very painful due to our sinful nature from lack of self-control.
3. Suffering to obtain the will of God and for the cause of Christ leads to strength, growth, and spiritual maturity. 1 Peter 5:10 (NIV) says:

   After you have suffered a little while, will himself restore you and make you strong, firm, and steadfast.

Chapter Eight: Forgiveness

1. Forgiveness is the expressed love of God towards mankind. (Matthew 6:14 and John 3:16). This act of God's love is what afforded us access to God our Father and Holy Spirit who empowers us to become sons of God (John 1: 12 and Acts 2: 37-

38). Forgiveness is proof that our sin debt was paid in full (John 19: 30).

2. Not only are we to love another, but we are admonished to forgive one another as we continue live in the eternal love of God (Ephesians 4:32).
3. True Forgiveness results in learning to let things go, Hebrews 4;16,

Chapter Nine: Provider

1. One powerful characteristic of God is His name Jehovah-Jireh, the Lord will provide is essential to our understanding of God and His love for us.
2. Knowing God as a provider requires that you remain patient during difficult times and hardships.
3. One of the greatest challenges as a man of God is not knowing or understanding where God is leading you but trusting and believing the Lord will provide and that is for us and the journey will end with positive results.

Chapter Ten: Worship

1. To worship God means to bow down, fall or lay prostrate in His presence.
2. When we worship God, we must worship in Spirit and in truth.
3. Worship is the result of coming to know the true and living God through an intimate relationship with Jesus Christ. Jesus Himself said, I am the way, the truth, and the life. No one comes to the Father except through Me according to John 14:6 (NKJV).

Finally, man of God you have reached the end of this book and the epilogue. An epilogue serves as a comment on or a conclusion to what has happened. It's the final section of a book that ends a particular story. What 's so awesome about God is that your story is still being written. Refuse to place a period at the end of your life and allow God to arrange the commas that will continue writing the book of your destiny. For God Himself, is the author and finisher of your faith and He has some amazing things to say about you.

Therefore, continue your journey of faith by connecting to a local church in your community that teaches the unadulterated word of God. Be willing to connect with other great men of God with like-precious faith to keep you accountable and on track as you walk in your purpose and fulfill your assignment. Disregard the lies of the enemy by pulling down strongholds, casting down arguments and every high thing that exalts itself against the knowledge of God. Satan is the Father of all lies and the battlefield he uses to wage war is with your mind.

In April 2022 I published a book titled *State Of The Mind.* The purpose of the book is to help individuals take a closer look at their present mindset that reveals potential barriers that prevent one from achieving a healthy, quality Kingdom life. Why not consider getting a copy, available through Amazon or www.keys4changeministries.com. Also stay connected by following me, Overseer Jay T. Harrison on various social media platforms.

Remember, time is given for the fulfillment of purpose. Utilize the traits that God has given you to fulfill His perfect will for your life. Until next time, I bid you well in that great word of peace, SHALOM!

Overseer Jay T. Harrison, Sr.

www.grace4purposeco.com

Made in the USA
Monee, IL
02 July 2023